Getting Dads on Board

Fostering literacy partnerships for successful student learning

Jane Baskwill

Pembroke Publishers Limited

For all the dads I have worked with over the years
—thank you!

Special thanks to the dads and kids who appear in the photos at the beginning of each chapter.

Note that pseudonyms for all fathers and their children have been used throughout this book.

© 2009 Pembroke Publishers
538 Hood Road
Markham, Ontario, Canada L3R 3K9
www.pembrokepublishers.com

Distributed in the U.S. by Stenhouse Publishers
480 Congress Street
Portland, ME 04101
www.stenhouse.com

We acknowledge the financial support of the Government of Canada through the Book Publishing Industry Development Program (BPIDP) for our publishing activities.

We acknowledge the assistance of the Government of Ontario through the Ontario Media Development Corporation's Ontario Book Initiative.

Library and Archives Canada Cataloguing in Publication

Baskwill, Jane
    Getting dads on board : fostering literacy partnerships for successful student learning / Jane Baskwill.

Includes index.
ISBN 978-1-55138-234-0

    1. Family literacy programs. 2. Education, Elementary—Parent participation.
3. Father and child. I. Title.

LB1528.B363 2009   372.6   C2008-907450-5

Editor: Kat Mototsune
Cover Design: John Zehethofer
Typesetting: Jay Tee Graphics Ltd.

Printed and bound in Canada
9 8 7 6 5 4 3 2 1

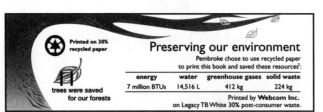

Printed on 30% recycled paper

Preserving our environment
Pembroke chose to use recycled paper to print this book and saved these resources[1]:

energy	water	greenhouse gases	solid waste
7 million BTUs	14,516 L	412 kg	224 kg

trees were saved for our forests

Printed by **Webcom Inc.** on Legacy TB White 30% post-consumer waste.

FSC
Mixed Sources
Product group from well-managed forests, controlled sources and recycled wood or fiber
Cert no. SW-COC-002358
www.fsc.org
© 1996 Forest Stewardship Council

[1]Estimates were made using the Environmental Defense Paper Calculator.

Contents

Introduction

When educators speak about parental involvement and the relationship between parents and the school, for the most part they are speaking about mothers. Mom is the picture that most teachers have in mind when they write notes home, send invitations to attend school events, telephone home about missed homework, or seek volunteers for class activities or trips. It is a picture rooted in school culture and past experiences, one that continues to focus more on the mother as the primary caregiver and school–home liaison.

However, in recent years, with changes to traditional family structures, there is evidence of greater involvement on the part of fathers in their children's lives. Fathers engage their children as they participate in building and repairing activities, hobbies, computer-related activities, sports, and outdoor recreation. They rough-house, play, and fool around with their children. They change diapers, take their children to medical appointments, and access parental leave on the birth of their children. A growing number of fathers read with their children, help them with homework, and give praise and support for schoolwork.

Even though fathers may be involved more in the lives of their children, this doesn't necessarily transfer to increased parental involvement in school on the part of fathers. Part of the reason goes back to the picture that schools, communities, and families themselves have of the parent likely to be willing and interested in being involved, or whose perceived responsibility it is to be involved with children's literacy learning. Thus, in most schools, fathers remain an important yet relatively untapped family literacy resource.

Research on the impact of involving fathers in children's literacy learning outcomes has shown the following:

- children do better academically when fathers are involved in literacy-related activities (Flouri & Buchanan, 2004)
- involving fathers early with their children's learning results in benefits to children in other areas: increased cognitive abilities, higher self-esteem, greater social competence (Ortiz, 2000)
- fathers' reading habits influence children's reading habits, choices, and interest (Gadsden, 2003)
- shared literacy activities strengthen the father–child bond (Stile & Ortiz, 1999)

Taking action to include both parents in a child's learning can make a positive difference to that child's achievement, motivation, and self-esteem. The combined influence of fathers and mothers can also make a significant difference throughout a child's schooling. The challenge remains for schools and teachers to put "dad" in their picture of family involvement and to find ways to make dads feel more comfortable taking part.

When speaking about "dads," I am using an expanded definition that includes biological fathers, stepfathers, foster fathers, grandfathers, uncles, partners, and male caregivers.

Researchers have been able to determine that a dad is more likely to become involved when

- his spouse/partner is actively involved in their child's academic learning and schooling
- he lives with the child
- his relationship with the child's mother is cooperative and positive. This is especially important when parents are divorced or separated.
- the school makes a concerted effort to reach out to fathers.

Researchers have also been able to identify what sorts of programs attract dads' participation. Dads are more likely to become involved in programs when

- school staff operate with a high comfort level when working with dads, and are open and accepting of dads' participation
- schools go out of their way to recruit dads and offer creative, innovative, and sometimes nontraditional ways (e.g., Bring a Dad to School Day) to attract dads
- there is community consultation with local dads about issues such as program content, recruitment, and design
- programs are interactive, dynamic, and built around hands-on activities
- publicity is explicit and directed at dads (the word "parent" is most often associated with moms)
- dads are invited to participate along with their children
- the literature used appeals to dads' interests and sense of humor
- learning experiences are connected to dads' interests and sense of humor
- dads and local community members help facilitate the program

Although more attention is being paid to research concerning dads, much more needs to be done at the school level. The development of an effective strategy for attracting, recruiting, and keeping dads involved in their children's literacy learning begins with the recognition on the part of the learning community that mothers and fathers both make contributions to their children's lives; that these contributions are in line with their individual interests, strengths, and identities; and that these contributions are both complementary and enriching to a child's learning.

What has been learned from successful projects is that one size does not fit all. It is important for schools and teachers to be aware of the differences between students and to celebrate and build upon them. Likewise, there is no single model for success when engaging dads in literacy-related activities. However, from the research and best practices in schools and classrooms, keeping in mind what attracts dads to programs, there are a number of strategies that teachers and schools can use to help attract dads.

The first chapter of this book presents an overall strategy for teachers to use to work dads into their current teaching practice. This strategy involves first taking stock of the ways teachers are already getting parents involved in their children's literacy learning, and then implementing the activities and events that make up the rest of the book. In this book you will meet eleven different dads (pseudonyms are used) and hear their true stories about specific literacy events that they participated in with their children. Each dad talks about a strategy he used and what he learned from this experience. These stories, along with the many stories yet to be told, can help teachers and administrators plan successful programs and activities aimed at getting dads on board.

With each strategy, I provide reproducible pages that are tools for your use in the classroom, as well as hand-outs to send home for parents. The latter are marked *For Dad* at the top left corner.

The chapters present a number of strategies for involving dads in their children's literacy learning. For each strategy, there are tools for the teacher, tips and activities to share with students and their dads, and a Dear Dad letter to send home with each student. Finally, Chapters 5 and 6 detail ways to involve dads in broadening the school–home connection and to increase involvement of the whole learning community, through workshops, take-home kits, and larger schoolwide events.

CHAPTER **1**   # Getting Dads Involved

Most teachers and schools recognize the importance of parental involvement. Parents are invited to fundraise, sit on school advisory councils, attend home and school meetings, and provide assistance for classrooms and special events. If you are like most teachers, you probably already try to involve parents in their children's literacy learning in some way. When you send a literacy bag home, respond to a parent's question in a pass-along book or journal, or send home notices or newsletters, you are fostering positive parental involvement. Yet, despite all your efforts, you may have noticed that you receive greater participation from moms than from dads. This is a common occurrence in many schools. Yet we know from the research that involving dads in their children's education can positively effect both dad and child. So, then, how do we develop an effective strategy for involving dads?

Taking Stock

A useful place to begin is to take stock of the ways you currently involve parents in children's literacy learning. Some things you are already doing (e.g., home literacy bags) can be tweaked a bit to appeal to dads. Sometimes by changing a graphic on a newsletter or changing the time you place a phone call will increase your contact with dads.

Use the charts on pages 13–17 to examine the parental classroom/school involvement activities you have already found successful. Record the activities you currently undertake that are aimed at parents. Indicate if there is evidence of dads' participation and, if so, estimate how many dads have been involved. This will provide you with some important data to help you make decisions about what is already attracting parents, who it is attracting, and how it can be modified with dads in mind. On page 10 are samples of the Parental Involvement in Schoolwork chart and the Parental Involvement in School Literacy Activities, filled in to this point. For reproducible copies of these charts, see Taking Stock: Parental Involvement in Schoolwork on page 13 and Taking Stock: Parental Involvement in School Literacy Activities on page 14.

Opportunities to Involve Parents in Schoolwork		
What I currently do	*Assigning reading to/with children*	*Have parents as helpers for Literacy Centres*
How often?	*Daily*	*2 days a week*
Target group	*Parents*	*Parents*
Are dads involved?	*Yes*	*No*
How many dads?	*2 out of 22*	*0*
Potential ways to increase dads' involvement		

Opportunities to Involve Parents in School Literacy Activities		
What I currently do	*Read-a-Thon*	*Family Literacy Nights*
How often?	*Once a year*	*Once a month*
Target group	*Parents*	*Parents*
Are dads involved?	*Yes*	*Yes*
How many dads?	*3 out of 22*	*10 out of 22*
Potential ways to increase dads' involvement		

In taking some time to take stock of what you are already doing, you will begin to think about ways these established practices can be shaped to get the dads in the family more involved. The information you record will help you gain insight into the roles dads already play in their children's learning (helping with homework, signing notes and permission slips, coming to school, etc.). You will also begin to see places where a new approach may be in order. Don't worry if you are not yet doing anything special to involve dads. Raising your awareness of what you might do is an important first step.

Once you have taken stock of what you are already doing, decide what small steps you might take that will be doable and easy to sustain. Following are samples of the charts for Communicating with Parents, Literacy Information Sessions, and Home Literacy Activities. For reproducible copies of these charts, see Taking Stock: Communicating with Parents on page 15, Taking Stock: Literacy Information Sessions on page 16, and Taking Stock: Home Literacy Activities on page 17.

Ways to Communicate with Parents

What I currently do	*Newsletters*	*Notices*	*Notes*
How often?	*Weekly*	*As needed*	*As needed*
Target group	*Parents*	*Parents*	*Parents*
Are dads involved?	*Unsure*	*Unsure*	*Yes*
How many dads?	*?*	*?*	*Not many; most responses by moms*
Potential ways to increase dads' involvement	*Have a Dad's Corner that provides dads with information and activities aimed at them*	*Use graphics that show dads as well as moms*	*Send notes/letters home specifically addressed to dad*

Literacy Information Opportunities for Parents

What I currently do	*Meet-the-Teacher Night*	*Parent–Teacher sessions*
How often?	*Once a year*	*Twice a year*
Target group	*Parents*	*Parents*
Are dads involved?	*Yes*	*Yes*
How many dads?	*8 out of 22*	*5 out of 22*
Potential ways to increase dads' involvement	• *Let families know session is for both parents* • *Have posters that show dads (and male caregivers) as well as moms with children*	• *Send home a survey to see what times are best for dads to attend* • *Send special invitations to dads*

Parental Involvement in Home Literacy Activities	
What I currently do	*Literacy Bags (take-home)*
How often?	*One bag each week*
Target group	*Parents*
Are dads involved?	*Yes*
How many dads?	*4 out of 22 dads signed logs*
Potential ways to increase dads' involvement	*Ask dads to help choose books*

You might not want to decide on potential ways to increase dads' involvement until you have completed reading this book; that's okay, too. You will notice a variety of skills and types of texts presented that relate to particular aspects of fostering children's literacy development (i.e. reading, storytelling, environmental print, writing and drawing). In some chapters, the skill or type of text is also combined with an issue. This double focus helps dads address obstacles or barriers that may be getting in the way of their successfully engaging their children in an activity. Helping dads address these issues can make for a more rewarding experience for dads and often provides a catalyst for raising other issues with which dads may feel they are in need of support. Keep the charts handy as you read through this book—as you come across each dad's story and the suggestions that follow, you can return to the charts as ideas occur to you.

Taking Stock: Parental Involvement in Schoolwork

Opportunities to Involve Parents in Schoolwork			
What I currently do			
How often?			
Target group			
Are dads involved?			
How many dads?			
Potential ways to increase dads' involvement			

Taking Stock: Parental Involvement in School Literacy Activities

Opportunities to Involve Parents in School Literacy Activities			
What I currently do			
How often?			
Target group			
Are dads involved?			
How many dads?			
Potential ways to increase dads' involvement			

Taking Stock: Communicating with Parents

Ways to Communicate with Parents			
What I currently do			
How often?			
Target group			
Are dads involved?			
How many dads?			
Potential ways to increase dads' involvement			

Taking Stock: Literacy Information Sessions

Literacy Information Opportunities for Parents			
What I currently do			
How often?			
Target group			
Are dads involved?			
How many dads?			
Potential ways to increase dads' involvement			

Taking Stock: Home Literacy Activities

Parental Involvement in Home Literacy Activities			
What I currently do			
How often?			
Target group			
Are dads involved?			
How many dads?			
Potential ways to increase dads' involvement			

How to Begin

Introduce the Process to Your Class

As you consider how you will get more dads involved, introduce the idea to your class. Once children are on board, they can be enthusiastic ambassadors for any activity. As families come in a variety of shapes and sizes, the topic of dads can be a sensitive issue for some, so it is helpful to know your families and to foster a climate in which children are accepting of the diversity of families that exists. Engaging your students in lessons on family diversity can help you get a sense of the diverse family structures from which your students come. This will help ensure that you provide opportunities for all family members to be involved.

It is important to acknowledge that there are many types of families, but to emphasize that, whenever parents get involved in children's learning, everyone benefits.

Introduce the Process to Dads

You can introduce dads to the important role they can play in their children's learning by inviting them to an information night. Send home a Dear Dad letter (see page 21) that gives a brief explanation, along with the date, time, and location. Also include a way for dads to indicate if they will attend. Include the information on your class website or in your newsletter to ensure the widest audience possible, and to act as reminders for both parents. Often, spouses or partners can be helpful in encouraging dads to attend.

Use the Dear Dad letter on page 21 to invite dads to an information night.

Plan the Process

Prior to the information session, you will need to decide what you will start with and how you will schedule the activities. There are several ways to do this that will lessen how daunting and overwhelming getting dads involved can seem. You might find it helpful to consider starting with one of the three ways listed below. There is no one right way. It is just a matter of finding the way that best works for you at the time.

Start with the Stories

Read through the dads' stories and select one on which to focus. You might choose to start with one that has a connection to an aspect of the curriculum or to a need you have perceived. Or you might simply pick one that you found informative or interesting, and want to share.

Start with the Chapter and Section Titles

The chapters in this book divide it into broad categories of literacy work with students. The chapters are divided into sections, each dealing with a more specific skill/text type in those general categories. Consult the table of contents to identify the general strategies and the specific skills highlighted in the chapter. You may want to begin with a familiar activity—like reading to children—that you are comfortable with, and about which many parents already have some knowledge and may have some experience.

Start with the Activities

Read over the activities and choose one that relates to an aspect of parental involvement that you are already doing, as identified on your Taking Stock chart. Or choose one that you especially like and want to try. In either case, the activity you choose should be one that can be easily tied into, or follow from, the curriculum. If you are able to link it to a structure you already have in place, so much the better.

Steps in Getting Dads Involved

Once you have decided on a place to start, the following provides you with a set of steps or actions common to getting dads involved, regardless of the skill or activity you have chosen:

1. Share the Dad's Story or Dads in Action example that illustrates the skill or activity you have chosen. These provide a talking point or a springboard into the activity and let dads know what other dads are doing. There are several ways to do this: in person, as part of a general information session, as a celebration, as part of the launch of the activity you plan, or through a newsletter, special notice, or current technology, such as a podcast or videocast. In fact, the more ways you share examples of dads involved in their children's literacy work, the greater likelihood you will reach more dads. In addition, when you reach out to a wider audience, you will help the wider school community, including other teachers and family members, to understand the importance of involving dads. This can aid in recruiting and supporting dads.

2. For each skill or activity you select, be sure to acknowledge the importance of the skill and how it can relate to children's learning at home and at school. The Dear Dad letters accompanying each strategy are great ways to introduce dads to a particular skill, and to support their use of it. Have a folder or duo-tang for each dad in which to house the letters and any reproducibles you might send home, or send an attractive fridge magnet with the first Dear Dad letter so it and subsequent letters can be displayed prominently.

3. Try to relate the skill to other age groups for dads who have children who are older and/or younger than the child in your class. It is often easier for parents to involve all siblings in an activity than to just include one.

4. Help dads understand how they can share literacy at home with their children—i.e., showing enthusiasm for literacy activities, talking about what they are reading or what they like to read, showing interest in what their children are reading, inviting their children to go with them to the library, sending positive messages about school and learning, etc. Encourage dads to think about the many ways they use aspects of literacy in their everyday lives.

5. Encourage dads to go with their instincts and capitalize on everyday situations that come up. Explain how literacy opportunities are everywhere. Remind dads to keep activities simple and enjoyable. Chances are, if they don't enjoy an activity, they won't be able to fool their children into thinking they do.

6. Help dads develop a repertoire of skills by providing them with activities they can do with their children. Some will reinforce what dads are already doing, while others will provide them with new skills and strategies to try. No matter how commonplace a skill or activity may seem, there are always ways to extend or expand on it, or to link it to some-

thing else. You already do this yourself as a teacher, and can share this ability with dads. The Dear Dad letters, along with the activities, materials, and additional information you provide for dads to use at home, will provide a consistent focus on involving dads. Organizing an occasional workshop on a particular topic might also become a tool you can use to spark additional interest or to respond to a particular need, thus providing another way to expand the dads' repertoires.

7. If you enjoy using new media and technology, you can develop a blog for dads. Include a series of podcasts and videocasts that discuss or illustrate the skill you want dads to focus on. The Dear Dad letters provide a ready-made script for your broadcasts. Solicit a dad who reads aloud well, and record him reading and interacting with his child. As more and more families have access to technology, it is becoming another tool that can help teachers get their message across to parents.

Building on the Strengths Dads Have

Regardless of how you plan to start, once you do you will gain invaluable insight into what works and what still needs to be done. It is important to stay positive and to work from the strengths dads have.

Not all dads are the same. They may have very different life histories, experiences, family structures, economic situations, and cultural or religious beliefs and practices. What is important is that you embrace this diversity and see it as an opportunity rather than a barrier. Here are some tips for getting to know each of your students' dads a little better, in order to gain important information that will help you as you design projects and activities that build on the strengths of the community of dads you want to involve.

- A great deal can be learned by speaking with and listening to dads and those who know them best—their children and their partners or spouses.
- Engage children in conversations about what they like to do with their dads. Try also to discuss how their dads help with their learning and what they would like to have their dads do.
- When reaching out to fathers who are not living with the child, be sure to have mom's support and be certain to examine the safety issues that may apply.
- Develop one-to-one relationships with dads. Consult with them about issues that affect them and how to remove barriers to their participation in their children's learning.
- Convince dads their participation is welcome and necessary. Help them to feel comfortable in your classroom or school. Consult with dads about how the school environment can be made to look and feel more welcoming to dads.
- Talk to moms about the importance of involving dads. This may be a sensitive issue for some moms, particularly for those who have experienced trauma or abuse. You will need to be mindful of the possibility that some moms will have difficulty including their child's dad in the learning process.

Dear Dad,

As a teacher, I know that dads want to help their child be a successful reader, writer, listener, and speaker, but might not be sure just what they can do to make a difference. I also know that when home and school work together, there is a greater chance for success.

Please join me for a Dads Workshop at school on the afternoon or evening of

_____, and find out about what you can do at home to help your child

in school. I know how busy you are, but this will be time well spent. At the

information session, I will share some activities you can do and strategies you can

use. I will explain the other activities I plan to offer dads throughout the year. I

would also like to find out from you what other ways I can help you help your child.

Finally, you will have an opportunity to meet and share information with other

dads.

If you will be attending the afternoon session, it will begin at _____ p.m. and end

at _____ p.m. The evening session will begin at _____ p.m. and end at

_____ p.m. The location for both sessions is _____.

I hope you will join me!

Sincerely,

Your child's teacher

PS: Please RSVP by returning the lower portion of this letter with your child by

_____.

✄——

❏ I will be coming to the afternoon/evening (please circle one) session.
❏ I am sorry I will be unable to attend.

Name: _____

CHAPTER **2**   # Dads Reading to Kids

Reading aloud is a practice that has many benefits for both dad and child. When dads read aloud to their children, it helps to bond parent and child and establishes a positive relationship around books and stories. It also sends the message that reading is important. Being read to helps children understand the purpose of printed text, builds their vocabulary beyond what they able to read for themselves, and provides the background for new readers to recognize new words because they know what they mean.

Reading aloud also provides a shared family frame of reference. In other words, dads and children have a shared experience that provides the material for "in jokes," spontaneous plays on language, and shared feelings. In addition, when dads read aloud to their children, they entice them into an exciting world of learning. This provides children with large amounts of information about the world and how it works, and results in the growth of children's general knowledge.

Finally, reading aloud, especially if dads lead children into discussing what is read, develops listening skills, gives the family an alternative form of entertainment, and provides a positive literacy experience for the whole family.

Be sure to remind dads that, whenever they can, they should read aloud to their children in person. However, as you will see in this chapter, there are other ways for dads to share stories with their children.

Reading Aloud

Reading aloud to children is often viewed as a parenting practice associated with the bedtime story. It is important to help dads look beyond bedtime for other opportunities to read aloud to their children.

Corran's Story

In the dads' stories, pseudonyms are used for all dads and their kids.

Corran is a farmer with two boys, age four and six. Like most young children, Lee and Christopher are very active and curious about things. They often accompany their dad to the barn to "help" with chores and each has a rabbit to look after. Corran tries to be in the house at bedtime so he can read his sons a story. When the children were younger, he started reading aloud to both boys at the same time, reading in Lee's bed one night, then Christopher's bed the next. But the boys grew older and their bedtimes changed, and there were times in the year when Corran was having to farm longer hours; by the time he came inside, both boys were asleep. He missed the established tradition of reading aloud to his children.

So I decided to read to them whenever I could—even though it wasn't bedtime. Lee, my youngest, didn't care. Any time was story time to him! It was Christopher who put up the biggest fuss. In fact, he became so mad at me that he refused to join Lee and me for any story. I felt pretty bad. I was pretty busy on the farm and couldn't just leave what I was doing to drive back to the house to read a story. One day, I mentioned [the problem with] Christopher to my dad and he suggested I read aloud anyway, even if Christopher wouldn't sit with us. He thought Christopher would likely hear the story anyway. He told me to read at the breakfast table, or at lunch, or anytime we were together. So I tried it and it worked. Christopher pretended to ignore us at first, but he was listening. I tried to make my reading exciting and talked about the pictures a lot. I would point out something funny or ask Lee if he could tell me what something I pointed to in the picture was. I started leaving the book on the chair I had been sitting in or on the table, and Lee would take it so he could look at the pictures. My wife said he would sit with the book before doing anything else. It wasn't long before Christopher started joining us. I actually think I learned to read better because I wanted to capture Christopher's attention. But I also think I saw a difference in Lee's attention. Instead of trying to stay calm, so they would fall asleep [as I would when reading at bedtime], I was able to be as noisy or as silly as I wanted. I could get them excited about the book.

What Can We Learn from Corran's Story?

Not only was Corran able to help his children learn that reading can happen any time, any place, but he also discovered that by changing location he was able to interact with the story differently. By making read-aloud time a more flexible and spontaneous event, he was also demonstrating that stories can become an integral part of everyday life.

He was able to choose a variety of stories beyond those he usually selected as being associated with bedtime and sleep. Being exposed to more tale types and genres helps prepare children to read more story types on their own. Corran was able to be more responsive to the demands of the text he was reading, making his read-aloud sessions more engaging and interactive.

Using Corran's Strategy

Tools for getting dads to read aloud:
For Dad:
• Dear Dad letter, page 26
For you:
• Appendix: Books to Read Aloud, pages 109–121

• Send your students home with the Dear Dad letter on page 26.
• Provide dads with information about why reading aloud to their children is important, along with some tips for making it a successful experience, using the Dear Dad letter on page 26.
• Share read-aloud class or personal favorites throughout the year. Learners of all ages enjoy a good read-aloud; reading aloud not only helps the literacy development of younger children, but benefits older children as well. Older children can improve their oral reading fluency by reading aloud to younger siblings or others in the school. Picture books can also be used as mentor texts to help students learn more about the craft of writing. Help dads understand that picture books are not just for young children, but can help the literacy development of older children when used as read-alouds. Send home a selected list to get dads started, and feature one or two new titles each month, or put selected titles in your class newsletter or on your website; see the list of Books to Read

Aloud on pages 109–121. You might also give the list to your school or local librarian.

- Be sure to let dads know that they can call on you for help when selecting read-aloud materials. Keep in mind that, although parents may have appropriate reading materials on hand, there is no guarantee that children will actually want to listen to them. Be ready to help those dads who may need more suggestions.
- Suggest to dads that read-aloud sessions can also be audio recorded for children to hear again and again.
- You can send home the Dear Dad letter on its own or along with a few books suitable for reading aloud. If you feel you don't have enough books to send home to all the dads in your class, you can create five Read-Aloud Bags to rotate among your families. Each bag contains four or five picture books for reading aloud, a laminated copy of the Dear Dad letter, and a Book Log. In the Book Log, dads record the books they have read and their recommendations for other books they have found that they like to read aloud. The books can be ones you have borrowed for this purpose from the school or public library, or could come from your classroom collection.

There are many excellent sources of read-aloud books on the Internet. Check out the Parents Choice and the Family Literacy Foundation websites for their suggestions.

Dear Dad:

Reading aloud to your child on a regular basis creates a special bond between the two of you, and also demonstrates to your child that you value reading. Here are some tips:

- Choose a comfortable spot where you both can settle in to enjoy the story. When reading picture books, be sure to sit side-by-side so you can both enjoy the illustrations.
- Select stories you and your child will enjoy. Pick books with interesting pictures and subject matter. You will do a better job with the reading if you like the book too!
- Read the selection to yourself first. That way you will know where you can add noises, voices, and special effects, or where you will need to read with more expression.
- Try not to rush the reading. Talk about why you liked the book, the part you liked the best, or the character that was your favorite.
- Leave the book where your child can read it again on his/her own.
- Encourage your child to join in the reading, especially if there are parts that repeat.
- If your child doesn't seem interested in the book, change the text by shortening it, changing the names of the characters to those of people your child knows, talking about the pictures without reading the words, changing the book's ending.
- Give your child a choice of read-alouds. Start with several you would enjoy reading and have your child choose among them.
- Make reading aloud part of your family's holiday tradition by reading a special story to go with the holiday.
- Read aloud material other than books. Anything with words that captures children's interest is appropriate for reading aloud.

Remember, Dad, read to your child at any age. It will be fun for you both!

Sincerely,

Your child's teacher

Video Read-Aloud

Dads often feel guilty when they can't spend time reading to their children. A recorded read-aloud is a great way to provide children with a read-aloud experience with dad even when he can't be there in person.

Be sure to remind dads that whenever they can they should read aloud to their child in person, but video read-alouds can provide a necessary alternative when they are unable to be home for extended periods of time.

Simon's Story

In the dads' stories, pseudonyms are used for all dads and their kids.

Shortly after the birth of his first son, Simon was deployed to Bosnia. Weekly communication with his wife kept him up-to-date with the latest news of his son's growth: his first tooth, his first smile, when he learned to sit up and crawl. By the time Simon returned home, he felt he had missed out on a lot. When his second son was born, Simon was around to experience all the firsts he had missed the first time around. He especially liked reading to James at bedtime, a practice that continued after James started school.

> But then, when James was around seven—right in the middle of us reading *Harry Potter*—I was sent to Afghanistan. I wasn't prepared for James' reaction. One night during our story time, about a week before I was to leave, James said, "But how will you finish reading me the Harry Potters?" I had promised I would read all of them to him when we started reading the first one. I was telling a buddy of mine about James' reaction and he said he saw a promo on TV about a project that provided dads in the military with a video camera and books, and they made videos of themselves reading the books which were then sent to their families. I thought this was a great idea and something that might just work for James, so I started making video recordings of the Harry Potters that I left with my wife to surprise James with.

What Can We Learn from Simon's Story?

Many dads, like Simon, find their work takes them away from home—serving in the military, away at courses, working for extended periods away from home or on business trips, or living permanently outside the home. Dads like these often miss out on being actively involved in their child's literacy learning.

Through Simon, we can see how important his bedtime story was to James. Both father and son valued their time together and the strong bond created by sharing stories. By recording the next book in the Harry Potter series for James and leaving it for him to watch, Simon demonstrated to James how much he valued books and reading. James enjoyed his dad's videos so much that he brought them to school, where they were shared with the whole class. As a dad involved in his son's literacy, Simon became a role model for his children and others as well.

Using Simon's Strategy

- Send students home with the Dear Dad letter on page 29.
- Share read-aloud class or personal favorites throughout the year; see the list of Books to Read Aloud on pages 109–121.

Tools for helping dads create video read-alouds:

For Dad:
- Dear Dad letter, page 29
- Tips and Techniques for Video Recording, page 30

For You:
- Appendix: Books to Read Aloud, pages 109–121

- Provide dads with a hand-out of tips and techniques for making their own read-aloud video recordings; see Tips and Techniques for Video Recording on page 30.
- If your school has a video camera, schedule recording times in your classroom or school library for dads who don't have a camcorder at home or who need help doing the recording.
- Put out a call to dads to find those willing to make audio or video recordings of favorite read-alouds. This might be a project your home-and-school association or parent group can take on. The recordings can be part of a growing library of read-alouds that families can sign out. Having such a library provides modeling for dads who are not confident readers, or for whom English is a second language. It also provides positive images of male readers.

Dear Dad:

Many dads find that circumstances mean they are away from home or separated from their children. If this is your situation, I want to share an idea with you—record yourself reading a favorite story. All you need is a video camera, or a computer and webcam, and you can still share the joy of reading with your child. Reading aloud to your child, even when you are away, sends a powerful message that reading is important and that this time with your child is something you highly value.

Attached is a separate sheet with techniques to help you in your recording. In addition, here are a few tips to make it seem almost like you are there with your child.

- Try to find a seat and a position to make yourself as comfortable as possible.
- Choose books that are age-appropriate, and that you enjoy yourself.
- Practice, and practice again. The more familiar you are with the story, the more you can concentrate on presenting it in a way that will engage your child's attention.
- Use eye contact and lots of facial expressions. Remember that it's not just about the pages and words you are reading, it's about YOU!
- Have fun! Your enthusiasm will be contagious, and your child will learn that it can be fun to read, because you are his or her reading role model.
- Remember that read-alouds can be for children of all ages. Novels and chapter books can also be recorded in the same way as picture books.

Remember: To create positive attitudes toward reading, create positive memories about books!

Sincerely,

Your child's teacher

Tips and Techniques for Video Recording

Book Selection

Choose books that are age-appropriate, and that you enjoy yourself. You can borrow books from your local library or from the school library. The librarian can recommend good books for reading aloud. In addition, local independent bookstores also have a good idea of books that appeal to particular age groups. Remember that read-alouds can be equally successful for older children as for little ones; novels and chapter books can be recorded in the same way as picture books.

In Advance

Read the book first. This ensures a book is age-appropriate and that you like it. If there are pictures, be sure to look at them carefully to see what you might want to point out to your child. Sometimes there is another story hidden in the pictures. Practice how you will read the book before recording.

Setting Up and Starting to Read

Find a comfortable chair and position the video recorder on a tripod or level surface facing you. If your video camera has a remote, use that to start recording. If not, start recording and then take your place in the chair; you might ask someone else to record you. Be sure to show the cover and state the title and author of the book.

Interaction

Think about ways to have your child interact and experience the book personally. Use your child's name and speak directly to him/her. Hold up the picture and point out things or ask questions: e.g., "Can you find…?" "Is this a…?" Having someone help you with the recording comes in handy, as they can zoom in on the page and then zoom out again as you move on. Anticipate that your child will respond; be sure to leave time, and to give an appropriate and encouraging response, before moving on.

Read with Expression

Use eye contact and lots of facial expressions. Remember that it's not just about the pages and words you are reading, it's about YOU! Change your voice and get into the reading by becoming each character or using your voice to make sound effects (e.g., the waves on the shore, a car driving, etc.). Your voice is a powerful way to hold your child's interest and attention.

Have Fun!

If you choose a book you like, this will come across in your reading. Your enthusiasm will be contagious.

Recording for Older Children

Novels and chapter books can also be recorded.
- As you read, talk about the meaning of the words that you think may be new for your child.
- Ask questions—"What do you think will happen next?" "What would you do if you were…?" "How do you feel about this story?"—and provide your own response before you move on.
- Suggest that your child view only one chapter a night. This will maintain your child's interest and, if it is a particularly good book, encourage your child to read it on his/her own.

Storytelling

Storytelling can be as effective a home literacy activity as reading aloud. There are many ways for families to make both of these activities part of their daily routines.

Storytelling has benefits for older children as well as younger ones. Storytelling

- helps spark children's interest, helps children create vivid pictures in their minds, and activates thinking.
- helps children connect events and concepts in order to better understand and later recall information and give it more meaning.
- takes information out of isolation and makes it more memorable. Children will listen to a good, relevant story because they will want to know what happens.
- builds listening and concentration skills, encourages creativity, motivates reading and writing, and instils excitement and interest in learning.

Because storytelling exposes children to a wide array of story structures and spoken language, it also increases their success as readers, writers, listeners, and speakers.

Berand's Story

In the dads' stories, pseudonyms are used for all dads and their kids.

Berand is a new immigrant. Although his spoken English is good, he is not confident with the written language. His wife speaks and reads very little English; therefore, almost all of the home literacy activities the school sends home are carried out by Berand. This includes the Literacy Bags sent home with the expectation that parents read every night with their children. Berand has four boys, ranging in age from five to twelve.

> When the bags first came home for the youngest, I tried reading every word of every book—after all, that's what they expected me to do. But I soon learned my son wasn't going to sit still for my poor reading. Some of the books had words in them I didn't know. I didn't do such a good job, so I didn't blame him if he wanted to go and play. [Our own] books we brought with us were a different story. I read them just right. So, I thought, what am I to do? One day the book that came home was a fairy tale—the one with the Three Bears. Instead of reading the story, I just started telling it. I did quite a good job, if I say so myself! Well, as soon as I finished, Hank wanted me to tell it again. So, I did. This time I changed a bit here and there and, to my surprise, that was an even bigger hit. Now, he wants me to read "my way" all the time! I still read aloud what I can, but I always tell Hank that, if he is a good listener, I will read one "my way" at the very end.

What Can We Learn from Berand's Story?

Berand shares a challenge with many parents—keeping a child's interest when carrying out home–school literacy assignments. English-speaking and recent immigrant dads alike may have to find their own style in order to engage their child and keep their interest to effectively carry out the expectations of teacher and school. They want to take part and recognize the importance of the activity, but they may have to find their own way to carry it out due to language or cultural differences. Berand has found a way to do what the school asks as well as hold Hank's attention. He is also benefiting his child by expanding his vocabulary, engaging his imagination, lengthening his attention span, and improving his listening skills.

Berand's strategy is one that many dads find useful. For a variety of reasons—including that a dad might feel pressure to compete with his partner's more animated reading style—dads often tell stories instead of read them. These tellings are often lavishly embellished with sound effects, exaggerated facial expressions, and even some physical play (e.g., tickling, wrestling). The addition of new characters—including the child, other relatives, and family pets—is not uncommon.

Using Berand's Strategy

Tools for helping dads in storytelling:
For Dad:
• Dear Dad letter, page 33
• list of Suggested Books: Tales to Tell from Books, page 34
For you:
• suggestions for Storytelling Sacks, page 35

- Send students home with the Dear Dad letter on page 33.
- Share suggestions for books that provide good stories for telling; see Suggested Sources: Tales to Tell from Books on page 34.
- Create a set of Storytelling Sacks for children to take home. Using props and familiar stories for retelling and playing storytelling games, dads can help children master communication, learn about language, and practice thinking skills. See Storytelling Sacks on page 35.
- In your newsletter or home book, share instructions for telling true stories from photographs:

Choose a selection of family photographs and talk with your child about them: when they were taken, who is in the picture, what the occasion was. Together select one picture. Ask your child what he/she would like to have you write about the picture, and print a sentence or two on a piece of white paper. As you write, talk about the letters you use and reread the words from time to time. Do not do this as if you are teaching, but rather as if you are reminding yourself of what you need to do as you write. Trim the white paper and arrange it with the photo on a piece of colored paper. When you and your child are happy with the placement of the photo and the text, glue them down the colored paper. Put up the page on the fridge or a bulletin board so you and your child can reread what you have written together.

Dear Dad:

Storytelling is an age-old tradition, and you don't need any special training to do it. In fact, you are likely already a storyteller! People tell stories all the time without really thinking about it. We recount things that have happened to us, share the plot of our favorite book or movie, and share the adventures of people we know (often our children). Sharing stories as a family is an enjoyable time and opens doors to better communication between you and your child.

Storytelling is a great way to build your child's language and vocabulary. It also builds self-esteem and confidence. Once you and your child learn some stories, storytelling can happen any time, any place—in the car, while waiting for an appointment, before bed. Older children will like learning tales to share with younger siblings, library groups, or other gatherings of peers.

Tell stories you have read and remembered, or recount events that have happened to family and friends. Tell stories about growing up. Feel free to add characters of your own (you or your child, for instance) to a familiar tale. Make your stories come alive by changing your voice or sharing roles with other family members. Here are some tips to get you started:

- Choose a story you both really like, maybe a story you and your child have read together.
- Read the story you have chosen a few times out loud to get the feeling, rhythm, and expression; to get to know the characters; and to remember the order of events or repetitive phrases.
- Make a map of the story. Fold a piece of paper into four boxes: in box #1 draw what happens first; in box #4 draw what happens at the end. In the remaining boxes draw memorable parts or scenes. Drawing will help you and your child remember the story.
- Keep it simple! Use only what's important to the story. Think about the five senses (taste, touch, smell, sound, and sight) to add interest.
- PRACTICE!! The only way to tell a good story is to tell it over and over.
- Tell it in your own words. You don't have to memorize it. Each time you tell the story it can be told differently.

Be enthusiastic and your child will be too! Have fun!

Sincerely,

Your child's teacher

Suggested Sources: Tales to Tell from Books

Here is a list of books to get you started. Don't forget about the many folk and fairy tales, too, as well as all or parts of longer books such as *Alice in Wonderland*, *Winnie the Pooh*, and *The Wizard of Oz*. Longer stories can be shortened, or told as serial, "to be continued" tales! Ask a librarian or local bookseller to help you find these or suggest others.

Why Mosquitoes Buzz in People's Ears by Verna Aardema
Cloudy with a Chance of Meatballs by Judi Barrett
The Mitten by Jan Brett
Flat Stanley by Jeff Brown
Stone Soup by Marcia Browne
Strega Nona by Tomie dePaola
The Gruffalo by Julia Donaldson (also *The Gruffalo's Child*)
Monkeys In My Kitchen by Sheree Fitch
Hattie and the Fox by Mem Fox
Millions of Cats by Wanda Gag
The Tailypo by Joanna Galdone
Something From Nothing by Phoebe Gilman
Mortimer by Robert Munsch
Tops and Bottoms by Janet Stevens
The Ghost-Eye Tree by Bill Martin, Jr. and John Archambault
Tikki Tikki Tembo by Arlene Mosel
Piggy Pie by Margie Palatini (also *Zoom Broom*)
The Day the Relatives Came by Cynthia Rylant
Where the Wild Things Are by Maurice Sendak
Wombat Stew by Marcia Vaughan
I Know an Old Lady (There are many versions of this old favorite.)

Storytelling Sacks

In each sack, include a note on how to play the storytelling game.

Magic Story Sack

Materials: Assemble an assortment of 6–8 objects in a cloth bag: small toys, such as a car or plastic figure; everyday found objects, such as a stone, a feather, etc.
How to Play: Start the story, "Once there was a magic _____." Pull an object out of the bag to finish the sentence. Together with your child, make up a story about this magic object.

Finish the Story

Materials: Assemble a variety of story starters (e.g., *One day a boy with a dog came to a bridge over a creek, and…*) on strips of card stock or on index cards. Put the story starters in a cloth bag.
How to Play: The object is for you and your child(ren) to tell a story together. Draw a story starter out of the bag, and begin the story by finishing the opening sentence. Invite the next person to add a sentence, and take turns until someone ends the story.

- An alternative way to play is to finish the opening sentence and to add as many as you wish or can before stopping and passing the story to the next storyteller. The next storyteller adds as many sentences as he/she wishes or can, and passes the story on, taking turns until someone ends the story.

Storytelling with a Picture Book

Materials: The picture book *The Mitten* by Jan Brett, a mitten, plastic animals. Other Jan Brett books that lend themselves well to this Storytelling Sack are *Gingerbread Baby; Town Mouse, Country Mouse; Goldilocks and the Three Bears; The Hat; Annie and the Wild Animals*.
How to Play: Using a real mitten and plastic animals, ask your child to choose which animal he/she would like to put in the mitten. Each time an animal is added say the following together:

> "It's frosty cold here outside.
> Let me in, let me in,
> where it's nice and warm."

Your child can retell the story of *The Mitten* to you, using the pictures of the animals in the story (photocopied from the book or downloaded from the Jan Brett website) and a mitten (real or cut out from paper). Your child can retell the story as it is told in the book, or make his/her own new version.

- Extension: You can go to the library and find out more about the animals in the story.

3

Dads and Kids Reading Together

Many types of print materials, in addition to books, find their way into homes. From an early age, children are surrounded by labels on products, catalogues, newspapers, and magazines, along with flyers and other mass mail. Outside the home, environmental print abounds. Goodman (1986) found that children as young as three years old were aware of print in their environment, and suggested that this is an observable sign of children's literacy development that is common to most learners.

This chapter focuses on everyday types of text with which families may be familiar. We must consider all text as potential literacy learning opportunities for dads to use. Through reading these materials, young children can gain reading confidence and learn to associate meaning with printed text. For both young and older children, these texts can be used to develop critical and visual literacy.

In addition to looking at ways of using the texts that surround us, the dads' stories in this chapter deal with issues that effect the quality or frequency of dad–child interaction: making the best use of limited time to spend with kids, grandparents' involvement in parenting, and working literacy into daily rituals. These issues often challenge parental involvement. The stories in this chapter can provide examples for dads struggling with similar issues.

Environmental Print

Because print is all around us, it is easy to find ready and inexpensive sources of literacy learning activities for dads. Focusing on environmental print can develop children's knowledge of the alphabet, and can help develop children's visual and critical literacy skills as well.

Mark's Story

In the dads' stories, pseudonyms are used for all dads and their kids.

Mark owns his own business. He works long hours during the weekday and often comes home long after his six- and nine-year-old are asleep. On weekends Mark tries to spend as much time as he can with his children. However, the weekends are usually taken up with family errands, sports and clubs for the children, and social outings with his wife. A lot of the time Mark spends with his children is spent in the car.

I want to help Missy and David with their school work, but I'm not able to. They have homework Monday to Thursday and I'm just not around then. But what I can do is play games in the car while we drive. A favorite is collecting words and signs that we see. When they were little, they would call out any store sign they could read—like McDonald's, Tim Horton's, Co-Op, Sears—or road and direction signs and symbols. As they got older, they started keeping a notebook of the signs they collected. Or sometimes I call out a letter and we look for as many signs as we can that begin with that letter, end with it, or have it somewhere in the sign. It's a lot of fun and I think they learn things too. Plus it makes the drive go more quickly. And I feel like I am helping with their school work.

What Can We Learn from Mark's Story?

Mark, like a number of other dads interviewed during my research, finds that having the time to spend with his children is an issue. He wants to help and be involved with their schooling, but his obligations at work do not make that possible during weekdays, when most school-related activities take place. Mark has found a strategy that allows him to use the time he has on the weekends and turn it into a learning experience for his children. The school Mark's children attend may never be aware of the contribution Mark is making to his children's literacy learning; however, Mark's story broadens our perspective on working with dads and designing activities that support dads' strengths.

Using Mark's Strategy

Tools for helping dads use environmental print:
For Dad:
- Dear Dad letter, page 39
- Activities to Try at Home: Environmental Print, page 40
For you:
- Car Games to Share with Dads and Children, pages 41–46

- Send students home with the Dear Dad letter on page 39.
- Use environmental print in your classroom on word walls, for math games, or for examining the meaning conveyed by signs and symbols. Enlist dads' help to collect samples (see Dear Dad letter, page 39), and share two simple activities dads can try (see Activities to Try at Home, page 40).
- Help dads develop a repertoire of learning games that they can play with their children in the car; see Car Games to Share with Dads and Children on pages 41–46. You can introduce a few games at a time to the children at school, and send a copy of the game home to dad on an index card that can be kept in the car.
- Create a Car Games for Dads and Kids book and send all the games home with your students in a Literacy Bag. After teaching the games to your students, you make a recording of you and the class playing the games that can be placed in the bag.

Dear Dad,

Environmental print is the print we see all around us: the labels on the cereal and peanut butter your child loves, the logo of a favorite fast-food restaurant, the stop sign at the corner. It is print we recognize from the colors, pictures, and shapes that surround it. Environmental print is usually the first print children recognize. Then they move on to reading the words, first without the color and then without the pictures and shapes. Recognizing environmental print makes children feel successful at reading and motivates them to read.

You can encourage your child to read environmental print. There are opportunities to point out print to your child, both inside and outside your home. As you prepare meals, read the labels of food items; when you run errands, read traffic signs and billboards; when you walk into a place of business (e.g., the bank, a restaurant, the sports arena), read and talk about the signs and the labels you find. Talk about the message the print is sending. Help your child notice what words or pictures are used; talk about the color; discuss who the sign or label is talking to. You will not only be stimulating your child's interest in asking questions about these common sources of print information, but will also be developing their critical literacy skills and their visual literacy skills.

I would like your help to bring environmental print into the classroom. Please collect familiar examples of environmental print with your child. Newspaper and magazine ads are an excellent source for print samples, as are coupons and labels on packaged foods. Please send in five of your child's favorites. We will be using these for various classroom activities.

Thanks for your help and interest!

Sincerely,

Your child's teacher

Activities to Try at Home: Environmental Print

Make a Book

- Staple some blank paper together with a colored paper or cardboard cover.
- Write the title of your book on the cover; e.g., *What's for breakfast?* (or *lunch* or *supper*).
- Glue labels from food packaging or pictures from ads in each page of the book.
- The book can be about one child or can be about the whole family, including any pets:

  Mom eats   _____.
  Dad eats_____.
  Fluffy eats_____.

- You and your child can make many kinds of books filled with your favorite labels. Older children can make books of environmental print for younger siblings or to donate to nursery schools, adult literacy groups, doctors' offices, or school.

Design Your Own Cereal Box

- Cover an empty cereal box with blank paper.
- On a separate sheet of paper, plan the design for your box. You might look at an actual cereal box to see the kind of information that is usually included.
- Draw your plan on your box.
- Make up a silly name for your cereal and use markers to add color.

Car Games to Share with Dads and Children

Who Stole the Cookie from the Cookie Jar?

This game gets everyone in the car involved with the familiar chant:

> *Dad*: Who stole the cookie from the cookie jar?
> _____ (child's name) stole the cookie from the cookie jar.
> *Child*: Who, me?
> *Dad*: Yes, you!
> *Child*: Couldn't be!
> *Dad*: Then who…

- As the game continues, another name is inserted in the chant. In the car, it is best to continue with names of other people in the car, in the family, or in the child's class.
- The game ends with the last person, who says "Who me?… Could be!"

A, My Name Is…

This alphabet game is adapted from a traditional ball bouncing chant.

> (*Letter*) my name is (*name that starts with letter*) and my best friend's name is (*another name that starts with letter*). We come from (place name that starts with letter) and we sell (*something that starts with the letter*).

> Example: *A* my name is *Albert* and my best friend's name is *Abe*. We come from *Annapolis Royal* and we sell *apples*.

- Continue in order through the alphabet, or skip around to find letters.

I Spy…

This traditional guessing game has been the staple on many a car ride.

I spy, with my little eye, something that _____

- Everyone tries to guess what the person has seen.
- This is made especially challenging in a moving car: players need to keep an eye out as they go, and the person who is "spying" should be prepared to give some hints.

I'm Going On a Picnic

This game asks players to figure out how the items named do or do not fit a pattern, and to add to the list.

- The first person to go sets the criteria

  I'm going on a picnic and I'm taking a _____ but not a _____.

  Example: I'm going on a picnic and I'm taking *apples* but not *oranges*.

- The next person chooses items to show they understand the pattern.

  Example: I'm taking a *book* but not a *novel*.

  Pattern: We are taking items that contain a double letter; *pp* in *apple* and *oo* in *book*.

- The first person confirms if the pattern has been followed or not.
- Players take turns until they show they know the pattern.
- Patterns can be colors (a lime but not a lemon), things that are outside (a barbecue but not a stove), things that begin or end with a particular letter, things that come in pairs (shoes but not belts), etc.

The Place Name Game

- A player begins the game by naming a town, city, province, state, country, etc. For example, the first player might give *Truro*.
- The next person must name a place that starts with the last letter of the previous one; for example, *Ottawa*.
- To keep the game collaborative rather than competitive, players try to keep the game going as long as they can. Experienced players know that this means choosing place names that end in letters that commonly start other place names.

Animal, Vegetable, Mineral

A variation of Twenty Questions.

- One player thinks of an object, a living thing, something to eat, something to play with, etc.
- The other players yes/no questions until they know what the first player has in mind.

Travel Alphabet Scavenger Hunts

NB: This game is for passengers only.

- Players keep their eyes open for things that start with each letter of the alphabet. They record what they have "collected" on a sheet of paper. Younger children can draw pictures of the items they see.
- One point can be allotted for each letter; a bonus point, for a total of two points, is given for the more difficult letters (*Q, X, Y, Z*). Most often, children will enjoy the game enough to play for no points.
- Variation: Lists of specific items for children to look for (e.g., someone on a bike, a traffic light, a grocery store, etc.) can be prepared in advance and placed in the glove compartment for use when desired.

Licence Plate Game

- Players see how many licence plates from different provinces or states they can find on their trip.
- Players write down the places, or check them off a list prepared in advance.
- Players can work as a team or individually. Play can last for one trip, or the search be extended to see how many can be found over that period of time. This can even become a family project.

Abbreviations

Play this funny word game with children of all ages.

- The object of this game is to make up funny abbreviations that different letter combinations can stand for.
- Players take turns being It.
- The person who is It names two letters; e.g., *F* and *M*. The letters can be an abbreviation or acronym that is commonly used or can have no meaning. (Letters can even be picked from the licence numbers of other cars!)
- Players take turns making up different terms that the letters could stand for. There is no right answer; the point is to be creative. For example, *FM* could stand for Fresh Mud, Fried Mittens, or Free Muffins.
- Play continues until there are no more ideas or until a pre-chosen time limit (three minutes is good) has passed.

Noah's Ark

- Players work their way through the alphabet, giving animal names that start with each letter from *A* to *Z*.
- Players can take turns with the letters in order. Or all players can get a turn for each letter.

You Can't Fool Me!

In this game, players take turns trying to fool each other.

- In turn, each player must state three "facts" about themselves. Two of the facts are true and one is made up.
- The challenge for the rest of the players is to discover which "fact" is made up. The player who stumps everyone is the winner.

Would You Rather…

- The first player selects a category; for example, *food*.
- The next player poses a question that offers a choice; for example, "Would you rather eat bugs or French fries?"
- The next player uses their choice from the question as the basis for another question: for example, *French Fries or ice cream? Ice cream with chocolate or worms?*
- The faster the turns are taken, the more challenging the game is. Topics can be serious or silly.

Car Opera

- Designate a time period for this game to last.
- For that time, when anyone in the car wants to say something, they have to sing it instead.

Let's Tell a Story

In this game, players collaboratively and sequentially create a story.

- The first player starts by saying "Once upon a time there lived…" and finishing the first sentence of the story.
- The rest of the players continue one or two sentences at a time until the story is finished.

Category Scramble

- The first player names a category; e.g., first names, last names, animals, countries, friends, feelings, foods, hot things, cold things, etc.
- Players take turns naming things that belong in the category. No repeats are allowed.
- When no one can think of anything else that belongs, the person who named the last item chooses the next category.

Three Nouns on the Go

- The first player names three nouns; for example, *mouse, bicycle, basket.*
- Players take turns creating as a sentence that contains all three nouns.

Print Instructions

The ability to follow printed directions is a life skill that benefits learners of all ages. Increasingly we find visual images are combined with minimal print to explain, say, how to assemble a product or how things work. Learning how to read this type of information is becoming an essential skill.

Dads can be encouraged to demonstrate this skill in everyday activities such as building something for their home or yard, putting together toys or household items, or making food for wild birds or supper for the family.

Micah's Story

In the dads' stories, pseudonyms are used for all dads and their kids.

Micah is in his late fifties and has one granddaughter, Sophie, who is eight years old. Micah and his wife are Sophie's guardian, and she lives with them in their suburban home.

> It took some getting used to, having a child around the house again. We thought we were through raising kids! Sophie is pretty quiet. She doesn't usually say much. When I would ask her if she wanted help with homework or if she would read to me, she'd just shake her head. At first I would get a bit annoyed. I thought she didn't like me. Then I thought she was just being stubborn. Then, one day, I brought a new barbecue home. It needed to be put together. There was an instruction book a mile thick. I was getting a bit frustrated because I had a few extra screws and didn't know where they belonged. Of course I hadn't checked the instructions before I started! Out of the corner of my eye, I noticed Sophie had her nose in the book. I tossed the screws over to her and asked her to see if she could figure out where they went while I worked on another section. Almost immediately she started talking. She showed me where they were in the book and where she thought they went. She also showed me how the handle looked in the book and said she thought I had put mine on upside down—which I had! We spent the better part of an hour putting that thing together and, when it was finished, Sophie and I read the directions for how to use it together. Now I know that the best way for me to talk something over with Sophie or to teach her something is by making something together—something that has directions I need help with.

What Can We Learn from Micah's Story?

Like many grandparents these days, Micah finds himself raising his grandchild. Though circumstances many vary as to why this is necessary, grandparents often find it difficult to step back into a parental role. Some find it hard to reconcile being both a grandparent and a parent, as they see these roles as being very different. Some feel out of step with the demands of today's schools, while others are embarrassed and afraid their grandchild will be treated differently by teachers and other children. Although the situation is more common today, there may still be a stigma attached with a child being raised by grandparents. Grandparents are often not considered to be effective disciplinarians or capable of helping a child with their learning needs. Yet many are very involved with the children in their care and are creative at finding ways to establish relationships with their charges that help their grandchildren with their literacy learning. Micah discovered that interacting with Sophie over the reading of directions was a strategy that not only engaged Sophie in a useful life skill, but also afforded an opportunity to talk, read, problem-solve, sequence, and focus on language and comprehension.

Some children can feel overwhelmed by parental help and may seem unwilling to allow parents to be involved with school learning tasks. Sometimes it is the parents' eagerness or impatience that is the problem. Other times it is caused by unreasonably high expectations that the child sets on their own performance; some older children may decide that it is not "cool" for them to have their parents' help. However, finding ways to establish a positive learning environment is key, and the first step is creating a bond between the adult and child.

Using Micah's Strategy

Tools for helping dads use print instructions with their children:
For Dad:
• Dear Dad letter, page 49
For you:
• Suggested Sources: Print Instructions, page 50

• In the classroom, introduce your students to the strategy for using assembly-line directions. Select activities in which the directions show, step by step, in pictures with minimal print, how to conduct a simple science activity, follow a recipe, or make a craft. Using an overhead or digital projector, talk about how to read this type of text.
• Send students home with the Dear Dad letter on page 49.
• In your newsletter or home book, share an assembly-line activity with dads; see Suggested Sources: Print Instructions on page 50.
• Send home an example of an assembly-line activity from one of the books from Suggested Sources: Print Instructions on page 50.

Dear Dad:

In class, we have been learning how to follow printed instructions. You can try these activities at home with your child, to help reinforce this skill.

No matter what the instructions are for, or where you find them (in a book, as part of a manual, online), look for the following features:

- Clearly drawn, simple illustrations for each step in the process.
- An easy-to-follow sequence of steps. Look for numbering of each step over one or two pages.
- Print used sparingly to label or explain.
- The materials to be used shown in the illustrations, along with the finished item.

If you have a project to work on together, you can make your own step-by-step instructions with your child using your own drawings or pictures from magazines. Another very effective way to create sets of assembly-line directions is to take digital photos of each step, print them (in color or black-and-white), and glue them on a sheet of paper or cardboard in sequence, with labels and a few simple directions.

Have fun assembling, fixing, or creating something with your child, and know that you are building your child's literacy skills at the same time!

Sincerely,

Your child's teacher

Suggested Sources: Print Instructions

Books

There are many wonderful children's books with just the right combination of step-by-step directions, pictures, and minimal print for assembly-line directions. Here are just a few:

Beading by Judy Ann Sadler—in the Kids Can Crafts series

Print-n-Stamp It by Laura Stickney—other books in the series: *Make-n-Gift It, Concoct It, Paint It, Transform It*

Activities for All Year Round by Angela Wilkes—other books in the Usborne Activities series: *Things To Make For Dads, Things To Make And Do With Paper, Monster Things To Make And Do,* and many others

Doodle Dogs, A Klutz Book—other books in the series: *Friendship Bracelets, Doodle Faces, Face Painting, String Games,* and the list goes on and on!

Other Sources

- A quick search on the Internet will give you many no-cook recipes that children like to make; for example, "ants on a log" made with celery, cheese spread, and raisins.

- The next time you play a favorite board game, actually go back and read the directions for play. You may be surprised to find that you have created your own family variations on a popular game!

- Family magazines often include recipes and craft ideas that are ideal for dads and kids to work on together.

Newspapers

Newspapers are a wonderful resource that can be used both at school and at home to support children's language, literacy, and critical thinking. Newspapers help children develop an interest in current events, stimulate their independent reading, and encourage them to pursue personal interests and hobbies.

Reading the newspaper together provides opportunities for dads and older children to come together over a current event and allows them to share issues, beliefs, and values in an informal, nonthreatening way. Everyday activities and routines, such as reading the newspaper, provide dads with opportunities to model literacy in use in a familiar context.

Don's Story

In the dads' stories, pseudonyms are used for all dads and their kids.

Don lives with his girlfriend and her daughter, Ali, who is seven. He doesn't enjoy reading books, but always reads the daily newspaper.

I'm pretty beat when I get home from work, but I still try to find time to spend with Ali. I used to tell her I would do something with her when I finished reading the paper. She didn't like waiting very much and when she was younger she used to put up quite a fuss. Then I would get mad and send her to her bedroom without doing anything with her. It was Ali's mom who said maybe she'd like to read the paper with me. *Why not?* I thought. She could read the pictures if nothing else. That's how we got started having what Ali called her "news time." It's something that has continued over the years. We started by looking for letters and numbers, and then people's names and words she could read. Now we talk about the news stories after we've each read them. It keeps me on my toes, because I have to explain some of the stuff behind the news. I even have to do research sometimes!

What Can We Learn from Don's Story?

Don enjoys spending time with his family, but also has an established routine that he finds relaxing and satisfying. Don discovered that, when he got home from work, he didn't have to choose between reading the newspaper and spending time with his child. He found a way to do both by sharing that experience with his daughter and making it a family literacy event.

We can see that that being in conflict with Ali for his own time and attention was not healthy for Don's family and that the behavior problem was beginning to escalate. By picking up on his partner's suggestion, Don was able to eliminate unwanted behavior and create an interest in reading about current events that is growing along with his daughter. Don recognized a good idea when he heard it and was willing to give it a try. It is evident that he came up with interactive games (letter/word searches, storytelling from the comic page, guessing at the story from the headline) that were quick and easy and didn't interfere with his overall reading and enjoyment of the newspaper.

When sharing this story with dads, acknowledge that it's okay to want to have some time to oneself. But point out that this strategy not only allowed dad to still enjoy his favorite activity, but also helped ease family tensions and redirect his child's behavior in a more positive way. In many classrooms, teachers use the newspaper for teaching. Whether using the newspaper for collecting word wall words, making books of letters, or writing their own articles and captions for a picture, dads can support their children's learning in a number of ways.

Using Don's Strategy

Tools for getting dads to read the newspaper with their children:
For Dad:
• Dear Dad letter, page 53
• Newspaper Games, pages 54–55
For you:
• Newspaper Activities for Class and Home, page 56

- Send students home with the Dear Dad letter on page 53. Distribute Newspaper Games, pages 54–55, to encourage dads to use their newspaper- reading time as an opportunity to play and learn with their child.
- If you have a newspaper unit planned for classroom work, you can incorporate some of the activities while sending home others; see Newspaper Activities for Class and Home, page 56.
- In your newsletter or home book, share a newspaper activity with dads; see Newspaper Activities for Class and Home on page 56.
- Some of your students' families may not have the newspaper delivered to their home every day. For these families, you can create a Literacy Bag. Include the letter and a few newspapers for dad and child to use.
- Approach your local newspaper to see if they would be willing to partner with you and provide day-old newspapers that could be sent home with each child for "homework," along with several tasks for dad and child to accomplish with that paper; see Newspaper Activities for Class and Home, page 56.

Dear Dad:

Newspapers are a wonderful resource that can support your child's language, literacy, and critical thinking. They can create an interest in current events, stimulate independent reading, and support the pursuit of interests and hobbies. Include your child in your daily routine of reading the newspaper. Start by introducing your child to how a newspaper works; let your child see why you find it so interesting:

Look at the parts of the paper together: headlines, articles, advertisements, comics, etc. Play I Spy and ask your child to locate these parts.

Read short, appropriate articles to your child: Select interesting stories to read aloud. Talk about the story together. This helps broaden vocabulary, and helps your child understand the variety of topics that could be included in their newspaper.

Share the news as you read the paper: A comment such as "Oh, look at this! Can you believe this?" will pique your child's interest. Look for items that relate to your child's life or interests. A simple, "I think you'll be interested in this" might be just enough to stimulate reading the article.

Give your child a section to read: Does your local paper have a kids section? If so, pull it out for your child and so he/she has something to read while you read the "grown-up" sections. Then sit down and read the comics, sports page, or whatever else interests your child together.

No matter what age your child is, the newspaper can provide lots of learning opportunities in an enjoyable way.

Sincerely,

Your child's teacher

Newspaper Games

Letter Search

Search for different letters of the alphabet. Throughout the various sections of the newspaper, your child can pick out type written in different sizes, colors, fonts (typefaces), and styles (**bold**, *italic*, etc.). As your child locates and then cuts out letters of the alphabet, he/she will discover the many ways that a letter can be written and still be that letter. These letters can be glued to paper to make an ABC poster or book.

Word Search

Go on a word search together. As your child begins to recognize words, encourage the search for the words he/she knows by sight. Use a crayon or marker to circle the words your child finds. You can create a word bank by cutting out the words your child knows and gluing them on index cards or piece of papers and storing them a decorated shoe box or envelope. Add new words and review the words in the bank together.

Focus on Pictures

There are many things to do with pictures from the newspaper:
- Look at the picture, cover it, and recall as much as possible.
- Make a scrapbook of pictures on the same topic.
- Make picture cards and play memory games.
- Make up a story about what might have happened before or after a photo was taken.

What's an Ad?

Introduce your child to the differences between articles and advertisements. Point out the drawings, the prices (with dollar signs), and the borders that often surround ads. Talk about the purposes of newspaper articles and ads: articles are intended to inform, while most advertisements try to influence us to buy something.

Comic Strips

Introduce your child to comic strips. Explain that the people in comic strips are characters, and the words the characters say are written in the bubbles, to introduce the concept of dialogue. Make up your own stories, and use the comics to tell your own versions.

Newspaper Activities for Class and Home

- Create a newspaper for the family or classroom. Children can report on the "news of the day," such as what was for dinner, any activities or games played, and who had homework.

- Use the pictures in the newspaper, the advertising supplements, and magazines to make an alphabet book or topic book. Students look through the newspaper for things that start with the letter/sound that they are supposed to focus on or are on the topic. They mount these objects on the appropriate page and bind them together.

- Make a time capsule as a special record of a birthday or holiday. Together, select interesting items such as the biggest headline, the weather, a sports event, a favorite cartoon, etc. Cut them out, and make a handwritten note about the day. Put them in an empty box and wrap it in newspaper. Put the date on the box and store it in a special place to be opened on the same date in a future year.

- Plan a party or a meal. Use the grocery advertisements and plan a menu. Decide on a budget and help your child select the items you need. Calculate how much they will cost.

- Create a scavenger hunt using the newspaper. This activity can be adapted to all learning levels. Use a page, a section, or the entire newspaper to create a list of items to find. For younger children, make the hunt broader: ask children to find a picture of an animal, the letter B, the color yellow, etc. The older the children, the more specific the list: the telephone number you would call to subscribe; the starting weekly cost for a home-delivered subscription of the newspaper; the name of the editor and publisher; a comic strip showing a working woman; the score from last night's hockey game, etc.

Catalogues and Flyers

Simple and inexpensive materials found around the house can be used as learning materials. Catalogue and flyers are readily available in most homes or can be obtained free from many businesses.

It is natural for parents to want to look to experts for the best ways to stimulate and support their child's learning. Although there are workbooks and learning games readily available, these can be expensive and, in some cases, poorly designed. Therefore, when you model how catalogues and flyers can be used as literacy learning tools, you help stimulate parents' thinking about using these everyday items in new and effective ways.

Gary's Story

In the dads' stories, pseudonyms are used for all dads and their kids.

Gary is a first-time dad in his late forties. Gary wants to make sure he does everything he can to make sure his son, six-year-old Andrew, will be successful in school. He worries that Andrew is a bit young for his age. Gary also worries that he isn't doing enough of the right things to help get Andrew ready for school. He questions his own ability to come up with appropriate literacy activities, and so he relies on the workbooks that are available from the store.

> One afternoon I was sitting with the Sears Wish Book catalogue. Andrew came and sat beside me, and I started playing a game with it. I just started doing it one day and now he wants to do it every day! One of us opens the book to a page—any page; then, with our eyes shut, Andrew or I will point to a place on the page. Then we make up a story about whatever we pointed to. Sometimes it gets a bit tricky—especially on the underwear page—and sometimes it gets pretty silly! I discovered that I can teach him words (the names of things) and colors, and how to make up stories and use his imagination, and we can even do sounds and letters, and, well, almost all the things that are in those workbooks—only they're way more fun the way we do it now!

What Can We Learn from Gary's Story?

Gary, like many dads, feels he doesn't have the training or knowledge to teach his child. He relies on mass-market learning materials that are not very exciting for either him or Andrew. Gary's story shows us effective use of very simple materials, like merchandise catalogues, that are readily at hand, to engage a child in a wide range of interesting and enjoyable learning activities. The positive response Gary repeatedly receives from Andrew when he employs this strategy gives him the confidence to create his own learning activities in response to Andrew's learning needs and interests.

Gary's story is also useful over a wide range of student ages. Using catalogues and flyer advertisements, older children can plan and "shop" for things they would like to have. This strengthens their numeracy as well as literacy skills. In addition, there is a problem-solving component to this work with catalogues, as children have to decide what the best buy is or what items they will eliminate in order to stay within their budget.

Using Gary's Strategy

Tools for helping dads use catalogues and flyers in literacy work:

For Dad:
- Dear Dad letter, page 59

For you:
- Catalogue and Flyer Activities for Class and Home, pages 60–61

- Send students home with the Dear Dad letter on page 59.
- The games and activities can be made and used in your classroom as part of a learning centre (Memory Card Game), an art activity (Crazy Collages), or a science or social studies unit by modifying the basic idea (Scavenger Hunt); see Catalogue and Flyer Activities for Class and Home, pages 60–61.
- In your newsletter or home book, share an activity with dads; see Catalogue and Flyer Activities for Class and Home on pages 60–61.
- Mount the directions for each game or activity on card stock or bristol board and laminate.
- Create a Literacy Bag with the materials for making each activity to send home. Encourage the students to bring in the games they make with their dads to share with the class.

Dear Dad:

Have you noticed the large number of catalogues and product flyers that find their way into your home? Instead of discarding these, you can make inexpensive literacy games and activities to play with your child.

- Make use of that junk mail. Everyone loves to open envelopes and scrutinize their contents. Save your junk mail and let your child open and read it.
- Use the weekly supermarket flyers to plan a meal or to calculate how much it will cost.
- Your child can use the words and pictures to make posters, signs, cards, and books.
- Make a floor plan of your child's room. Have your child use catalogues and newspapers to "furnish" the floorplan.
- Write down a list of groceries that you commonly buy each week. Have your child look through the flyers, comparing the prices of the items at each store. Together, you can cut out the items with the lowest prices and add them up for a total grocery bill. For an extra challenge, have your child look for corresponding coupons for the items. How much money will you save using the coupons?

These activities are just a beginning. You will likely think of some other ones. If you do, please share them with me, as I am always looking for new ideas!

Sincerely,

Your child's teacher

Catalogue and Flyer Activities for Class and Home

Memory Card Game

This concentration game can be constructed with two copies of an old catalogue, a deck of playing cards or index cards, scissors, and glue.

Set Up: Select identical images from the two copies of the catalogue and cut them out. For smaller children, images of toys or recognizable faces work best. Older children might do well with more detailed pictures. Keep each pair of images together until the catalogues have been thoroughly searched for usable pictures. Glue each image to a playing card or index card.

To Play: You'll need a minimum of two players or two equal teams.

- Shuffle the cards. Lay them out in rows of 5 or 6 cards each.
- Each side turns over two cards at a time, revealing the images below.
- If the images match, the team keeps the pair. If they do not match, the player turns them back over and the other side takes its turn.
- The game is over when all of the cards have been collected. The player (or team) with the most pairs collected is declared the winner.

Classroom Variation: Instead of playing the game, children make their own deck to take home.

Scavenger Hunt Game

This game calls for a numerous collection of catalogues with different themes: e.g., building supplies, pets, garden, etc.

Set Up: Find a number of specific products inside the catalogues and write each item on a separate index card or piece of paper.

To Play: Place the catalogues in a pile in front of your child. If more than one child is playing have a list and pile for each.

- Call out the name and the price of a specific item listed on one of the cards.
- At a predetermined signal (a bell, a squeaky toy, the word "Go!"), the players sort through the pile and find the listing that matches the item. The first player to locate the item wins.
- A single player can work against the clock by using a timer.

Crazy Collages

Use scissors, glue, and paper to attach pictures cut out of catalogues to bristol board. Old catalogues can be the basis for some humorous combinations of images. For example, your child might put a dog's head on a fashion model's body, and add a few toy UFOs in the background. Or you and your child might construct funny sayings by cutting out individual words and phrases. Older children might create entire comic book scenes or funny fake advertisements.

Dioramas

You will need small cardboard boxes (shoe boxes, tissue boxes, or cereal boxes will work) and stiff paper, like card stock, for mounting the images. Some may want to use small wooden craft sticks or toothpicks with pieces of floral foam or modeling clay as a base. Help your child decide on a background image and layer other images from back to front as you create your scene together. Many catalogues cater to a specific theme—e.g., the holidays—which means plenty of appropriate images for a display.

Where's Waldo (or Mickey, or Winnie,…)?

Set Up: Together, decide on a character, animal, or particular object to hide in a collage. Make a collage on a quarter sheet of bristol board, using an assortment of images from catalogues, incorporating a picture of your selected character. Vary the size and color of the images, and glue them in various positions—upside down, some facing right and left, etc. Fill the bristol board with images. (Depending on the age of your child, you can cut out images in advance from which your child can select.)
To Play: Send the collage to school so your child can see if his/her classmates can find the object or character you have hidden on the page. Encourage your child to try out the activity first on family members and friends.

Plan a Garden

You will need garden books, blank paper, and markers, along with an assortment of seed and bulb catalogues. Make a blank book with your child by folding four sheets of white or colored paper in half and stapling on the fold. Write MY GARDEN JOURNAL on the cover and decorate. Cut out pictures of favorite flowers or the flowers and/or vegetables your child would like to plant in the garden. You might first plan out the garden on a sheet of paper and label the garden map with what you want to plant.

CHAPTER **4** **Writing and Creating Together**

The process of learning to write begins in early childhood and continues into adulthood. The positive writing experiences children have at home and in school contribute to their interest, skill level, and enjoyment. When young children observe that adults are writing in order to accomplish real tasks, they learn the value and function of writing. When older children receive a consistent message from home and school that values writing, they learn that writing is an important life skill.

When you provide opportunities for parents to interact with children during home writing activities, you help parents to develop an understanding of what children are learning at school and to provide children with important models and demonstrations of positive parental engagement with writing. These activities can also support the learning outcomes that are part of your writing program.

This chapter describes how to involve dads in their children's writing by providing strategies and activities through which dads and children can observe, explore, experiment, and create with writing at home. The ideas for involving dads in their children's writing focus on writing for authentic purposes, stimulating the composing process, and increasing dads' comfort level so they can be positive role models for their children.

Writing Activities

Some children do not seem to be interested in learning to read and write, and it can be difficult for parents and teachers to get them to engage with it. Many older children struggle with writing, finding it difficult or tedious and something they only associate with school.

Encouraging authentic writing activities draws on students' personal knowledge, fosters creativity, and heightens excitement about language and learning. Authentic writing tasks also cultivate students' confidence in their writing, as they make connections between school and home. Providing dads with suggestions for engaging children with interactive and authentic writing helps them tap into their children's interests in enjoyable ways.

Alex's Story

In the dads' stories, pseudonyms are used for all dads and their kids.

Alex is a single dad with one child, five-year-old Paul. Alex works at a local store and arranges his hours so he can be home when Paul gets home from school. Alex is concerned that his son doesn't seem to be interested in sitting down to practice writing or spelling.

Paul is a going concern. He would much rather hold a bat than a pencil. I guess he's a bit like me in that way. I found a way though, quite by accident, to help him practice his letters and sounds without him really knowing it! One evening after supper, while doing the dishes, I noticed we were low on dish soap. Paul was playing in the kitchen, so I asked him, since my hands were wet, to write *soap* on the shopping list on the fridge. He was so happy to do this for me that he wanted to know what other things we needed so he could write them down too! I learned that if I want Paul to practice his writing, it goes better when it is fun and for a purpose—like the shopping list.

What Can We Learn from Alex's Story?

Alex knows Paul very well. He recognizes his son's need to be active, and he also is aware of his learning preferences. He can relate to these from his own experience. However, he also recognizes the importance of getting Paul to practice his letters and sounds.

Alex's strategy appeals to Paul's current level of development, and can provide a bridge to more formal learning activities. Because Alex is tuned in to his child's learning needs, he is able to capitalize on spontaneous learning events and make them part of his family's everyday literacy learning activities. When communicating with dads, explain the importance of capitalizing on everyday situations—encourage them to go with their instincts and keep activities simple and enjoyable.

Using Alex's Strategy

Tools for getting dads involved in authentic writing activities:
For Dad:
• Dear Dad letter, page 65
• "Dad and Me" Journal Template, pages 68–69
For you:
• Authentic Writing Ideas for Class and Home, pages 66–67

• Help dads develop a repertoire of authentic writing activities they can do with their child. Send home the Dear Dad letter on page 65 to explain why dads' involvement is important. The general tips and suggestions will help dads encourage writing in their homes.

• You will find a variety of ideas that can be incorporated into your writing program; see Authentic Writing Ideas for Class and Home. As you plan your writing lessons, keep this idea list handy and insert those activities that support your teaching. For instance, when you introduce journal writing to your children, send home the "Dad and Me" Journal Template (pages 68–69) for dads to use to make a blank journal to write in with their children. Ask dads to send the journals to school with their children on a designated day for sharing.

• Look for ways to incorporate these activities in other areas of the curriculum. For example, the Dads in the Kitchen cookbook can become part of a nutrition/healthy foods unit; The Nature Walk or Listening Walk can be worked into your science lessons.

• In your newsletter or home book, share an activity with dads; see Authentic Writing Ideas for Class and Home on pages 66–67.

Dear Dad:

You are a powerful role model for your child. Involve yourself in your child's writing in an enjoyable and natural way, and writing will become a much more meaningful experience for your child. Here are a few suggestions of ways you and your child can enjoy writing together:

- Send notes to family and friends.
- Write letters to your child and encourage him/her to write back.
- Make lists: e.g., wish lists, lists of things to take on a trip, a list of people to invite to a birthday party, lists of supplies for a building project, etc.
- Make signs and labels for things your child creates or owns.
- Make a family job chart.
- Mark events on a calendar.
- Keep a journal together.
- Take pictures of an interesting activity and use them to write a story.
- Make a Writer's Box for your child: together, paint or decorate a box and stock it with pens, markers, pencils, crayons, assorted paper (lined and unlined, colored and white, various sizes), ink pads and stamps, sticky notes, envelopes, etc.
- Bring writing materials with you, in a resealable bag, whenever you go to the doctor's office, out to dinner, or for a long ride in the car.
- Create a family communication centre where you can leave notes for each other: e.g., a small corkboard or a mailbox made out of a shoebox.

Most importantly, have fun writing together!

Sincerely,

Your child's teacher

Authentic Writing Ideas for Class and Home

Dad and Me

Using the template, kids create a blank book. This becomes a journal in which they keep observations and reflections on the activities they do with their fathers. Those who have digital cameras can take photos of events and activities to illustrate their writing.

Our Own Picture Book

Using templates based on predictable picture books, dads and kids create their own versions of the stories starring themselves.

Dad's in the Kitchen

Start a Dad's in the Kitchen cookbook. Dads and children find foods they like to prepare together, and write or type special recipes for future use.

Our Trip

Dads and kids can be the family trip recorders for day trips or long vacations. Disposable or digital cameras can be used to take photos of family activities. The pictures can be put in sequential order in a scrapbook, then captions or stories explaining the photos (who, what, where, when, why, how) can be written. A similar album can be compiled using any family photos.

How To…

Dads and children make a video showing how to do something: how to build something, how to cook something, a video tour of their area, how to shop, how to play a game, etc. With parents' and students' permission, this can be shared with the class.

Where in the World

Invite dads and children to come to the library and research a place they wish they could visit: e.g., castles of Scotland, volcanoes in Hawaii, bat caves in Texas, Mount Everest, pyramids in Egypt. After researching, dads and kids plan the trip together. Older kids can help prepare a trip budget.

Animal Favorites

Invite dads and children to go to the library and take out books on an animal they want to learn more about. Together, they write and illustrate a book about their animal and read it to the family at a special dinner or over dessert.

Letters to the Hospital

Dads and kids write letters and cards to send to the children's wing of a hospital, the veterans' hospital, or a nursing home. Suggest they get others in their community or local school involved.

The Play's the Thing

Have a session where dads and children write a play they can perform for a family member on a birthday or as a holiday gift. Suggest they include scenery and costumes. If a video camera is available, they can record it for showing at a special time.

A Family Story

Dads and children think of an incident or adventure and write a family story together, incorporating a setting, characters, problem and solution, and events leading to the end. Encourage them to add details and dialogue. Encourage exaggeration and imagination.

Nature Walk

Dads and children take a walk around the schoolyard, neighborhood, park, or beach, carrying notebooks and pencils so they record items they collect. They collect specimens and then go home and write about their treasures and where they were found. Finally, they work together to add illustrations.

Listening Walk

In this variation on the Nature Walk, dads and kids write down what they hear while walking around the schoolyard, neighborhood, etc. They write a Listening Book or poems about the sounds they heard.

Cloud Watching

Dads and kids go cloud watching in the schoolyard or a nearby park. In a notebook they sketch the clouds and write down what they see in the cloud shapes. As a class, create a Cloud Book, with each dad-and-child pair illustrating a page with paints, markers, or cotton and glue. The completed book can be placed in the classroom or school library.

"Dad and Me" Journal Template

Instructions

Cut out each two-page spread. Stack the spreads and fold down the middle. Staple along the fold.

	My "Dad And Me" Journal This book belongs to
Books we like to read	**Things we like to do**

Games we like to play	**Here is a picture of my dad and me**

Places we like to go	**Food we like to eat**

Drawing

Drawing a story while reading it aids in comprehension, and can lead to discussions about the characters, plot, or setting—things that may get overlooked when the focus is on the reading alone. The drawing provides a talking point for parent and child about the story that can be returned to throughout the reading. Interactive drawing is not only highly motivating and enjoyable, but it also allows children to express complex thoughts and feelings they may not be able to convey in words. Drawing can also be used as a bridge to writing. It can be a way for children to organize their thoughts, stimulate thinking, and convey ideas in an alternative format.

François' Story

In the dads' stories, pseudonyms are used for all dads and their kids.

François has four children—three boys and a girl, ranging in age from four to fourteen. His is a very busy household, with children going off to clubs and sports almost every afternoon or evening. He and his wife have chosen to send their children to English school to avoid the long drive to the Francophone school. As a result, they are teaching their children French at home, in addition to supporting their children's literacy learning in English. François is most concerned about his youngest boy, Henri, who is in Grade 3. Henri isn't interested in reading. He would much rather draw. He says that he finds reading boring.

> I was really getting worried, and even asked the school what we should do. The school sent home some books they thought he would like and suggested we take turns reading to each other. But Henri wasn't interested in doing that either. Then one day, we were both in the living room and Henri was drawing. I watched as he drew a basketball court and the players on both teams. They weren't elaborate drawings or anything, just stick figures with different colored shirts and numbers, so you could tell them apart. As he drew, he told the story of the game. He showed the movement of the players with dotted lines, and the movement of the ball with arcing lines. It was obvious he had a story in mind and he was retelling it in pictures. This gave me an idea. Later I brought out one of the books he had brought from school. I asked Henri to draw the story, just as he had done earlier with the basketball game, as I read the chapter. After a few pages, I asked Henri to read and I took over the drawing. This approach seemed to intrigue him. He had quite a chuckle over some of my additions to the drawing, as I did with his. We went back and forth, taking turn reading and drawing. It was the most enjoyable chapter we had ever read together, and the best part was that Henri started to really get into the story.

What Can We Learn from François' Story?

François picked up on an activity his son already enjoyed—drawing—and used it as a bridge to reading. Because the activity was made interactive, it was manageable for both François and Henri. The switching from reading to drawing after every few pages ensured that neither task became overwhelming.

François also was able to take advantage of the books the school had sent home. Teachers who know their students' reading interests or preferences can be helpful sources of books that will likely capture a reluctant reader's attention. The books provided François with a starting point. The combination of a good book with an interactive and creative reading activity was just what Henri needed to pique his interest and get him into reading. The enjoyable time Henri spent sharing the reading with his dad was another factor in the success of this activity.

Using François' Strategy

Tools for getting dads involved in interactive reading and drawing activities:
For Dad:
• Dear Dad letter, page 73
For you:
• Fishbowl Strategy for Interactive Reading, page 72

- Use the Fishbowl Strategy on page 72 to demonstrate to your students how the interactive reading and drawing strategy works.
- Once the students understand how interactive reading and drawing work, send home the Dear Dad letter on page 73. Note that you can delete the PS if the letter is going home without the book and drawing materials.
- Include copies of the Dear Dad letter on page 73 with selected books and some drawing materials in Literacy Bags that can be sent home on a rotating schedule.
- See Authentic Writing Ideas for Class and Home on pages 66–67 and adapt the activities to include or focus on drawing instead of writing.

Fishbowl Strategy for Interactive Reading

- Choose a volunteer from your class.
- Sit side-by-side so you both can see the book you are going to read, and at the front of the classroom so the rest of the class can see.
- Decide on a signal to use to indicate you want to take a turn reading or a break from reading: raising a finger, tapping an arm or shoulder, passing the book, etc. If you want to be really creative, use a noisemaker or squeaky toy as a signal.
- Start reading aloud from a book you have selected.
- You or the student will give the signal to switch the reading duty. Be sure to point out to the class when the signal is given and what is happening.
- Continue taking turns reading until you have demonstrated the strategy several times.
- Repeat with another student.

Drawing Variation

Do the same demonstration using drawing.
- Select a student volunteer (preferably one who likes to draw), and decide on a signal to use.
- Sit side-by-side at the front of the classroom.
- Read aloud from a poem, a chapter book, or a picturebook that has a lot of description.
- Whoever is not reading is drawing an aspect of the story—the characters, setting, action, etc.— until one of you gives the signal.
- Continue taking turns reading and drawing until you have demonstrated how the strategy works.

Dear Dad:

Interactive reading is a cooperative and enjoyable way for you and your child to share the reading of a book. It is a very helpful strategy to use if your child is reluctant to read or lacks reading confidence. It can also just be a way to add a little something new to your reading time. Here's how it works:

- Decide on the book to be read.
- Explain to your child that you will both share the reading. Decide on a signal that will tell when you are ready to read, or when you have read enough and want the other person to take over.
- You and your child take turns reading.

When your child is taking a turn reading, you should signal to take over when you notice he/she is struggling a bit or at the end of a page. There is no hard and fast rule for how much each person should read. The important thing is to make it enjoyable so your child will look forward to the experience.

A variation of interactive reading is to incorporate drawing with the reading. Most children love to draw and will usually participate enthusiastically. Here's how it works:

- While one person reads, the other draws some aspect of the story (e.g., the characters, the setting, the action). You don't have to be an artist. Stick figures and simple drawings are best.
- Take turns drawing and reading, using the signal to switch tasks.

The drawing provides a talking point for you and your child to refer to as your reading continues. The drawing will help your child remember the story and will also allow you to see if he/she is understanding what you have read.

Sincerely,

Your child's teacher

PS: In this Literacy Bag, I have included a book that I think you could use to try this technique with your child, along with a small package of drawing materials. Please return it by _____.

Storyboarding

Children sometimes find the task of writing daunting. They may have an idea or a complete story in their minds, but do not know where to start to get it on paper. With routine writing tasks such as journaling, children may have difficulty sustaining the activity over a period of time. Storyboards are a way to help children organize print and visual information. They help with structure and sequence, and are a way for students to plan out their final product.

Photos and pictures can also be used to stimulate writing. They help children focus on the visual cues in an event and recall the thoughts, emotions, people, and places in more vivid detail. Visuals can also be catalysts for creative storytelling, when children are encouraged to make up a story of their own from pictures in magazine or newspapers.

Martin's Story

In the dads' stories, pseudonyms are used for all dads and their kids.

Martin is a radio broadcaster and the father of twins, a boy and a girl aged ten. His children are in Grade 5 and have a teacher who wants her students to write every day at home in a writing journal. The twins complained they didn't know what to write about. They said they hated writing, and always pleaded to be allowed to do it after they got home from their activities, rather than before sports or Scouts. However, it would get late and the writing would be left for morning, when it would end up going unfinished. The twins were threatened with not being allowed to go to their activities, but neither Martin nor his wife, Anna, believed this was the right thing to do. Things were getting more and more stressful for the family.

> I was getting desperate. The teacher was sending notes home, the twins were digging in and refusing to do the writing journal, and Anna and I were at our wits end. So I asked myself, if I had to do this journal at their age, what would I write? Where would I get my ideas? It came to me one night when I had our old family photo albums out. I thought that, if I could get the twins to look at the photos, they might find something to write about. Well, it was amazing. They were so excited and animated as they recalled where they were when the picture was taken, how old they were, and other details not visible in the photo. They laughed and went on and on. This was what they needed—they needed a starting point, something to spark their memory and their imagination. I took a few pieces of paper and, as they were reminiscing, I wrote down what they were saying. I did the same for each of them. I gave them each their "story" and suggested they use this as a starting point for their journal. They were so surprised that they went off and actually did their journal assignment. Now, whenever they are stuck for a writing idea, they go back to the old photos.

What Can We Learn from Martin's Story?

Homework can be a pressure-filled time in most households. The more insistent a parent is, the more resistant a child becomes. Martin knew the journaling assignment wasn't going away. He also knew that the problem would likely get worse before it got better. His strategy was to put himself in his children's shoes, to try to view things from their perspective, and then to relate that to what he would have done in their situation. By asking himself where he would get ideas to write about if he were their age, he was able to think past the assignment itself and problem-solve rather than escalate the conflict. This led him to find a solution that was supportive and creative, and that modeled how other difficult learning situations might be approached in the future—head-on rather than by avoiding them.

Regardless of a child's age, attitudes toward learning tasks that a child finds difficult, or new tasks they are uncertain about, can lead to resistance. This can become a habit of resistance or avoidance. If children can learn to view these times as problem-solving opportunities, they will develop strategies they can apply throughout their lives.

Using Martin's Strategy

Tools for helping dads use visuals to stimulate writing:
For Dad:
• Dear Dad letter, page 77
• Storyboard Template, page 79
• blank book made up of Single Photo Pages, page 78
For you:
• Single Photo Page Template, page 78
• Storyboard Template, page 79
• Class Photo Storybooks, page 76

- Incorporate Martin's strategy into your social studies or language arts curriculum, by creating Class Photo Storybooks, see page 76.
- Send home the Dear Dad letter on page 77 in a Literacy Bag, along with a Class Photo Storybook, a copy of the Storyboard Template (page 79), and a blank book made up of Single Photo Pages (see page 78) with a blank cover made of card stock.

Class Photo Storybooks

- Choose a theme for the books.

- Have students bring in one photo each. You may have to take a photo for a child who doesn't bring one.

- Have the children share their photos with a partner or in small groups.

- Each student temporarily attaches his/her photo to the top of a blank piece of paper, using a piece of removable tape on the back of the photo.

- In small groups, students lay out their photos in order and number their pages for future reference.

- Individually, each student decides what to write about his/her photo. Some students may want to make notes or write a rough draft before writing their text below the photo.

- Give each group a copy of the Storyboard Template. Students share what they have written with a partner or in their original small groups. They combine and order their photos using the Storyboard Template, making any changes needed to their writing or to the order of the photos.

- Make a photocopy of the Single Photo Page Template for each student; distribute the blank pages to the working groups. Each group transfers their photos and writing onto the pages.

- Help each group order, collate, and staple their pages together into a Photo Storybook, leaving a blank page for a cover. Have the group put a title, their names, and an illustration on the front cover.

Dear Dad:

As well as a vehicle for sharing memories and good times with your family, photos can be a great way to initiate writing for your child. At school we have been learning how to make Photo Storybooks, using a storyboard to help organize our ideas before writing. Enclosed in this Literacy Bag is an example of one of our class stories.

You can make photo stories with your child using family photos you have on hand. In the Literacy Bag, you will find a blank storyboard for you and your child to use to plan out your story, along with a blank book to transfer your story into. Here's what to do:

- Choose a theme for your book: e.g., growing up, family traditions, friends, pets, summer vacation, school events, holidays, etc.
- Select five or six photos that go with your theme.
- Using the enclosed blank storyboard, help your child decide the order in which the photos should go. Write the page number on the back of the photo.
- Together, decide what to write about each photo. Write this on the storyboard space that matches the number on the back of the photo.
- Attach one photo and transfer the accompanying text to each page of the blank book, following the storyboard plan.
- Give your book a title and write your child's name and yours on the cover. Decorate with another photo or a picture drawn by your child.

Your finished creations can be used as gifts on birthdays or holidays, or as remembrances of family trips and events. If you and your child would like to share your creations with the class, please send your finished books to school with your child. We will be making a display to feature them all.

I hope you have a wonderful time sharing family stories and memories with your child.

Sincerely,

Your child's teacher

Single Photo Page Template

Storyboard Template

Title Page

Page 1

_____

_____

_____

Page 2

Page 3

_____

_____

_____

Page 4

Page 5

_____

_____

_____

Bookmaking

Teachers know that, when making a book is part of a writing project, interest usually increases along with students' acquisition of language skills. Because making books can be highly motivating, producing a product that is attractive and well-written becomes a self-imposed objective. This is likely because the writing and illustrations that are inside are treasured items.

When teachers are book art enthusiasts, they convey this passion to their students. When this enthusiasm is shown at home, making books can be a shared experience between parent and child. Bookmaking is an activity that dads can initiate on their own. It is a way to build children's enthusiasm for and confidence in writing their own books. The act of making a book has a lot of appeal for children of all ages. It is also an activity that can be done with all the children in the family at the same time.

Tony's Story

In the dads' stories, pseudonyms are used for all dads and their kids.

Tony is the father of three girls, ages six to thirteen. He feels like the odd-man-out in a household of all females. Therefore, he tends to leave decisions about the raising of the children to his wife, depending on her to tell him what she wants him to do.

> The girls came home with a flyer from the school about a bookmaking workshop for dads. Dads could bring their children with them and make blank books. When Martha said I should take the girls, I thought she was kidding—me, make books? No way! But she said the school wouldn't have invited dads if they didn't think we could do it. I still wasn't sure, but the girls were all over it, bugging me to take them. So we went. They had all the directions and all the stuff. We made a couple of different kinds of books and took home the directions and materials so we could make a few more at home. The girls loved the books. They had all sorts of ideas about putting stuff in them. I really got into it, though I didn't think I would. In fact, it was my idea to take some of the yarn and glue it around the outside edge of the cover to make it a little fancier. Well, the girls thought that was just the best—they thought I was the best too! It felt really good. I don't think I'll be so nervous going to a dads workshop the next time. My wife was right; the school knows what it is doing when it comes to this stuff.

What Can We Learn from Tony's Story?

Like many dads, Tony wants to be involved with his children, but doesn't usually initiate activities. He defers to his wife when it comes to school activities and events, as she has most of the contact with the school. When his wife finds an activity that he is likely to enjoy doing with his children, makes all the arrangements, and reminds him when to go and where, Tony feels enough support to get involved. He goes on the class field trips or helps with any building projects. The bookmaking workshop was a new venture for him but, since both his wife and the school were confident he would be able to do it, he went.

Often, dads need a sort of barometer for gauging the trustworthiness of an activity or event. By providing support, specifics, and a nonthreatening environment for new activities, you can boost a dad's confidence to the point where his involvement is seen as low-risk to his self-esteem as a parent.

Using Tony's Strategy

Tools for helping dads make books with their children:

For Dad:
• Dear Dad letter, page 82

For you:
• Bookmaking Activities for Class and Home, pages 83–85

- Send home the Dear Dad letter on page 82 to underline the learning opportunities that go along with making books with children.

- The activities presented in Bookmaking Activities for Class and Home on pages 83–85 can be shared with your students as alternative forms of representing when responding to picture books or novels, when reporting on information in science or social studies, or as an art activity that features the art of the book.

- Older students can learn how to make each book in a literacy station. Younger students can be teamed with an older buddy to make books. The books can be used as invitations for dads to come to a special event; to share information with dads about an aspect of literacy or other area of the curriculum; or as part of a display for dads in the hall outside your classroom during parent–teacher meetings or home–school events.

- Copies of directions from Bookmaking Activities for Class and Home, pages 83–85, can be sent home when there is a link to something you are taking up in class. For instance, when learning about the environment, multiculturalism, or conflict resolution and peaceful schools, send home the directions for making Wish Scrolls. You can share the messages in the scrolls as a class activity and display the finished scrolls hanging from a tree branch you have spray painted white or silver.

- From time to time, post a new set of directions from Bookmaking Activities for Class and Home, pages 83–85, in your class newsletter in a Just for Dads column. Request that dads help their children create a book on a specific theme to add to the classroom display or as part of a curriculum project.

Dear Dad:

Reading to your child every day is the most important thing you can do to help your child become a reader for life. A great way to keep children interested in reading is to help them create their own books. The best thing about making books and booklets is that you can make up a story, share information about your favorite subject, or delve into researching a subject you want to learn more about—when the book is finished there is a sense of satisfaction and pride.

Creating a book with your child is an activity that you can make as simple or as complex as you like.

- All you need to start creating your book is paper. Use a notebook or create your own blank book by taking several sheets of paper and binding them together. Punch holes along one side and use brass fasteners or yarn to bind the pages together. You can also use an inexpensive blank bound book or photo album. Photo albums can be great because they already have plastic sleeves that can help protect the pages of your book.
- When creating your book, you can make up a new story from scratch or retell an old favorite with your own illustrations. Provide crayons or markers so your child to draw simple pictures to go along with the story.
- Another alternative is to cut out the pages of an existing book. Glue selected pages or parts of a page in a blank homemade book or notebook; add new pages and drawings to create different storylines from those originally in the printed book. If you personalize the story by gluing in photos of you and your child (or family members and pets), you and your child become central characters in the story.
- Recycled materials such as brown grocery bags, cardboard from cereal boxes, wallpaper pieces, and used greeting cards, along with other odds and ends you find around your home, can be made into books of all kinds of shapes and sizes.

After you and your child have finished creating your homemade book, don't forget the most important part of the activity—reading your book together. Since your child helped to create it, he or she will likely want to spend time with you reading and rereading the book.

Sincerely,

Your child's teacher

Bookmaking Activities for Class and Home

Wish Scrolls

This easy-to-make book is based on the Ethiopian Wish Scroll. The scroll and its cardboard carrying case can be given to someone special after being filled with birthday, holiday, friendship, or any other joyful greetings. It can be worn around the neck or hung on a door, bulletin board, or tree branch.

Materials:

1 cardboard toilet-paper tube
24" (60 cm) piece of yarn or macramé cord
2 beads or buttons (large enough to allow the yarn to pass through)
1 strip of paper 3" (7.5 cm)wide and as long as you want: e.g., adding machine tape, strip cut
    from a brown paper grocery bag or wrapping paper
Wrapping paper, paint, or colored paper
Scissors
Glue
Sharp pencil

What to do:

- Cut the colored paper so it covers the tube. Glue the paper around the outside of the tube. Or you can use paint, markers, or crayons to decorate the outside of the tube.
- Tie a bead to one end of the yarn using a double knot. The bead should be inside the knot.
- Use a sharp pencil, nail, or hole punch to put a hole on one side of the tube. Be careful not to punch the hole too close to the top edge. Thread the end of the yarn opposite the bead through the hole. The bead will stop it from going all the way through.
- Punch a second hole opposite the first and push the end of the thread through the hole, going from the inside of the tube to the outside. Tie a bead around the end of the yarn in the same way as the first bead.
- Pull up the yarn from the centre of the tube so the tube is suspended from a yarn necklace.
- With a pencil, write some wishes for the person you plan to give the scroll to. You can also write wishes for the Earth or for your school. Decorate your wishes by drawing pictures or making the letters ornate.
- Roll up the scroll and slide it into the tube from the end opposite the yarn.

Stick and Elastic Binding

This book is easy to make and looks great too. You can use craft sticks, twigs, or dowels to support the spine of the book; this version uses a colorful unsharpened pencil.

Materials:

8 sheets of 8 1/2" x 11" (21.5 x 28 cm) paper in white or assorted colors
2 pieces of lightweight cardboard or cover stock: e.g., cardboard from a cereal box
1 elastic band (medium size)
1 unsharpened pencil, old marker, or pen
Hole punch

What to do:

- Select 6 to 8 sheets of paper.
- Cut cardboard covers slightly larger than the paper you are using.
- Position the paper between the covers.
- Punch two holes through all the layers of the book.
- Wrap the elastic around the pencil and thread the other end through the holes, starting from the top.
- Bring the elastic up through the other hole from the back and wrap that end of the elastic around the other end of the pencil.
- Gently fold back the cover and make a crease so the book will open more easily.

Note: You can make any size book, depending on the length of the pencil or the stick you choose.

Accordion (Concertina) Fold Book

As a child, almost everyone learned how to make a paper fan. This book is based on that simple folding skill. An added feature is that the book, when completed, can stand up so all the pages are visible at once. Accordion Fold Books can make an interesting presentation format for school projects and reports.

Materials:

1 long, narrow strip of paper: you can measure, fold, and cut a sheet of paper in halves or thirds, then glue the strips together

Bristol board, card or cover stock, or the front and back panels of a cereal box

Glue stick

Scissors

Sheets of scrap paper

Ribbon or strip of colorful cloth

What to do:

- Fold the paper strip in half.
- Take the edge of the top layer and fold it back to meet the centre fold.
- Turn the strip over and do the same to the other side. Depending on the length of the paper, you may want to add folds; make sure that the folds alternate directions, making a fan pattern.
- Place a piece of scrap paper under the first "page" of the folded paper, to protect your work surface. Lightly cover the page with glue. Place the book glue-side down on one corner of the cardboard cover, leaving a narrow cardboard border around the edges of the paper. Trim.
- Trace around the edge of the cardboard cover on a second piece of card stock. Trim so you have a cover of the same size as the first.

- Protecting your work surface with scrap paper, lightly cover the last page with glue. Place the book glue-side down on the second cardboard cover, leaving a narrow cardboard border around the edges of the paper, as before. You should now have a "fan sandwich," with the folded paper between two cardboard covers.
- Add a ribbon or strip of colorful cloth as a decorative way to hold your book closed.

The Step Book

This is an easy-to-make book that looks great when it is finished. Each page lifts up to reveal whatever you choose to put underneath. As you go down the "steps," the area beneath the flap gets larger.

Materials:

3 sheets of 8 1/2" x 11" (21.5 x 28 cm) paper
2 child-size shoe laces or pieces of yarn cut in 12" (30 cm) lengths
Hole punch
2 beads (optional)
Cardboard strip 1-1/2" (4 cm) wide: as a guide to measure

What to do:

- Lay the pieces of paper one on top of the other. (If you use colored sheets, you will get a rainbow effect!)
- Place the cardboard strip at the top of the page and slide the middle and top sheets down so they are just below the guide.
- Move the cardboard guide to the top of the next sheet and slide the top sheet of paper so it is below the guide. Remove the guide, leaving the 3 sheets of paper positioned about 1 1/2" (4 cm) below each other.
- Carefully, keeping the pages as they are, turn them over. You will see 3 steps at the bottom.
- Place the cardboard strip at the bottom of the new top page. Fold the top of the page back to meet the top of the guide and crease.
- Reposition the guide and fold the next page down to meet it. Do the same with the first page.
- Hold the pages together and open them on the fold enough to slide in the whole punch. Push the punch in as far as it will go and make a hole on the fold, punching through all the layers. Do the same on the other side.
- On each side, thread one of the shoelaces through the whole. Make the ends even and tie in a double knot. (You can add a bead to decorate before tying the knot.)

CHAPTER **5** # Workshops and Take-Home Kits

Included are descriptions of projects that have been successfully implemented. These Dads in Action segments will give you a thumbnail sketch of each initiative.

Dads are an untapped resource in many of our schools. Teachers and schools have a great opportunity to provide dads with activities and strategies that will help them become more involved with, and supportive of, their children's learning.

The suggestions and activities in this chapter focus on two models for helping dads become more effective in their parent–child literacy interactions: workshops and take-home kits. Although planning and assembling these activities take more time and resources to organize, the benefits to dads and children are well worth the effort. Often schools are looking for innovative ways to involve parents. Focusing on dads may be an idea others in your grade level or school will want to get on board with as well.

Workshops

Workshops, whether one-off or a as part of a series, are a great way to get dads involved. The most successful workshops have the same key elements that contribute to their success. When designing workshops:

- Make them factual: Dads want information. They want to know "how to." Whether it is about reading to their child, going on a nature scavenger hunt, or motivating reluctant readers, dads want to know what they can do. They also want to know why their help is important for their child.
- Keep them active: Pace is important with workshops for dads. To keep both parents and kids involved, break up the workshop into shorter segments and vary the content or task in each segment.
- Ensure there is a hands-on component: Try to design each session to provide an opportunity for dads to practice the skill on which you are focusing, or to try out the game, craft, or activity—either alone with their children or in small groups.
- Include discussion: Some researchers advise that activities for dads should not contain too much discussion. I have found that discussion is an important feature of running a successful workshop for dads, as it helps develop a sense of community and a network of support, something dads are often missing when it comes to their children's literacy development and schooling. If you plan discussion, try to keep it open and allow for diverging topics, and you will find dads will become enthusiastic participants.

Some things to do *before* the workshop:

- Carefully consider the school-year schedule, also noting larger community events. You won't be able to avoid all scheduling conflicts, but try to find the optimal time.
- Give dads ample time to arrange their schedules. Send home invitations well in advance. Be sure to ask dads to register so you will some idea of how many are coming. Follow up with a reminder between the first announcement and the workshop date.
- Plan the workshop agenda and estimate how much time you will need for each item. Be sure to build in some flexibility, so you can adjust times in order to finish on time. This is important if you want dads to come to another event in the future!
- Gather the materials you will need. Quantities will depend on how many participants you have. Have extra materials on hand for unregistered participants. Make enough copies of any reproducible you may need.
- Set up the room you will use. If you use your classroom, be sure to enlist the children's help getting the room ready.

The more organized you are, the more smoothly the workshop will go, and the less time it will take in the long run. One final thing to remember—stay positive. Don't be discouraged if only a small number of dads show up. It sometimes takes a while for an idea to catch on. Be persistent, solicit input from the dads who do attend, and try again—word will spread. And keep in mind that the children of the dads you do reach will reap the benefits of your efforts.

Video Read-Aloud

See Chapter 2: Dads Reading to Kids, page 27.

Invite dads to a video workshop if you feel the strategy would be a good fit due to their work or family situation. You may want to make the workshop a family event and invite spouses along so they can help with the recording. Share Simon's Story (page 27) and show a video you have made of a dad reading a book aloud. Have lots of read-aloud books on hand and provide time for dads to read aloud to other dads and receive supportive feedback. Distribute and go over Tips and Techniques for Video Recording, page 30. If you have access to several video cameras, set up stations at which dads can go to record their reading. If funds for this project are an issue, ask dads to bring their own DVD or VHS tape for recording.

Silly Stories

See Chapter 2: Dads Reading to Kids, page 32.

Hold a Silly Stories event for dads and children. Engage a local storyteller to open with a few interactive stories that invite participation. Demonstrate simple home storytelling techniques: telling stories from the daily comics, telling "When I was a boy…" stories, making up a story from props, etc. Have dads and children try them out.

Car Games for Dads and Children

See Chapter 3: Dads and Kids Reading Together, page 38.

Send invitations to a dads-only event and, depending on your finances or how creative you want to be, consider holding the event on a school bus! If a bus is out of the question, make a large decorative mural of a car to get everyone in the mood. Teach the dads simple chants and rhymes (see Car Games to Share with Dads and Children, pages 41–46), like "Who took the cookies from the cookie jar?" or alphabet chants such as "A my name is...". Supply coffee and donuts, and distribute copies of Car Games to Share with Dads and Children, pages 41–46.

A How-To Evening

See Chapter 3: Dads and Kids Reading Together, page 48.

Hold a workshop session for dads and their children, focusing on using print instructions to develop literacy. Set up six to eight stations with directions and materials. The directions should show, step-by-step, in pictures with minimal print, how to conduct a simple science experiment, follow a recipe, or make craft. Dad and child collect the directions and materials, work together at empty tables provided for that purpose. See Suggested Sources: Print Instructions, page 50, to source crafts and activities.

Catalogue Carousel

See Chapter 3: Dads and Kids Reading Together, page 58.

Invite dads to a Catalogue Carousel. Have stations set up around the room with a variety of activities that can be done with catalogues; see Catalogue and Flyer Activities for Class and Home, pages 60–61. Give dads and children ten minutes to sample the activity at each station. Copy and send them home with complete directions (Catalogue and Flyer Activities for Class and Home, pages 60–61). After the Catalogue Carousel workshop, ask dads to send in any additional activities they have created for using catalogues and flyers. Publish some of these ideas, with the dads' permission, in the class newsletter or on your website.

Secret Messages

See Chapter 4: Writing and Creating Together, page 64.

Send home a "secret message" to dads, inviting them to an evening of "make and take." At the workshop, provide an assortment of directions and materials for creating secret messages. "Magic" invisible ink and the means to reveal it can be made of nontoxic ingredients readily available: lemon juice/heat to reveal; baking soda and water/paint over with grape juice concentrate to reveal; white crayon/paint over with poster paint diluted in water to reveal. Have the dads write a message to leave in their child's desk or mailbox.

Interactive Reading

See Chapter 4: Writing and Creating Together, page 71.

Invite dads to a session about interactive reading; see Fishbowl Strategy for Interactive Reading, page 72. Demonstrate turn-taking when reading aloud, and how each dad and child can invent their own signals when one or the other is ready to take over the reading of the book. Also demonstrate how drawing can be incorporated into the activity, with the help of a colleague or willing parent (you may want to practice a little with this person prior to the workshop). Use the overhead projector and a well-chosen book to show the dads how it is done. Be sure the drawings are not too elaborate and that they look like anyone could do them. Take turns with the role of reader or drawer. After a few minutes, give out some paper and have the dads draw while you read. Send home resealable bags that include drawing materials and a book chosen for each child in your class for dads to borrow; include a copy of the Dear Dad letter on page 73 for those who were unable to attend the session.

Photostory Workshop

See Chapter 4: Writing and Creating Together, page 75.

Invite dads and their children to a photostory workshop. Ask them to bring with them up to five family photos that have a theme (e.g., Christmas, celebrations, food, pets, etc.) or were taken of the same event (e.g., a vacation, a birthday party, a renovation project, etc.). Take the dads and children through each step to create their stories:

- Use a storyboard to sequence the photos (Storyboard Template, page 79)
- Write a few sentences about each photo on the storyboard.
- Transfer the photos and text to a blank book you have provided: staple or sew together six copies of the Single Photo Page Template, page 78, with a card stock cover.

If your school has a computer lab, dads and children can take their template to the computer to type up and print out.

Bookmaking Workshop

See Chapter 4: Writing and Creating Together, page 81.

Invite dads to bring their children to a bookmaking workshop. Fifteen dads with their children is a manageable number. In advance, prepare a set of directions (see Bookmaking Activities for Class and Home, pages 83–85) for each dad, along with the materials for each child to make all the books. It is also a good idea to have the paper cut to the correct size for each book. At the workshop, explain how the session will work. Keep the introduction to a minimum so most of the time can be spent doing. Let the dads and children decide which books they want to make and what book they will make first. They will be able to complete two or three blank books in approximately 45 minutes. Dads and children can take home the directions and the materials for the books they didn't get a chance to make.

Dads in Action: Picture It, Dads!

Picture it, Dads! was supported by an Adult Literacy grant from the Canadian Council on Learning.

The Picture It, Dads! project engaged dads of children aged three to seven in a series of six Saturday morning literacy workshops. This initiative was developed in response to surveys conducted with rural dads in Nova Scotia. Although they expressed a desire to be involved with their young children's literacy development, they also expressed a lack of confidence in their knowledge and abilities. The six workshops focused on positively effecting the attitudes and literacy practices of participants and their families, while also attempting to change stereotypically held views toward dads (i.e., dads aren't interested in being involved; literacy is mom's responsibility).

Each workshop provided dads with ideas and activities for supporting early literacy development, a support network of other dads, and guided practice with their children. Take-home bags were given to the participants at each workshop. The bags contained:

- the picture book that provided a touchstone for each workshop theme
- a blank book for recording home literacy stories and developments
- a booklet of activities that springboarded from the touchstone book
- a bibliography of related books available at the local public library
- a package of materials to use at home

Each workshop focused on specific goals for dads and children. Workshops ran for two hours with the time broken up to include a read-aloud modelling session with dads and children, TalkTime (time for dads to engage in discussions around books and literacy activities while the children made a craft with help from an early childhood facilitator), and Bookmaking Time (time for dads and their children to use various computer technologies to make a book that starred each father–child pair, from a template inspired by the touchstone book).

The dads evaluated each session and made suggestions and recommendations regarding content and organization for subsequent sessions. The workshops achieved a number of things. The dads began initiating literacy activities between workshop sessions. They shared these activities with the other participants and facilitators. They gained confidence in their own ability to create new activities and to carry out the activities designed for them. They also bonded with their children around books and reading, and were rewarded for their efforts by the positive responses from their children. They found a way to put their own stamp on literacy activities in their home, which raised their comfort level. They no longer felt they had to compete with their wife or partner, or with their child's teacher. They raised the profile of dads as literacy partners. Participants felt that what made these activities successful was

- Receiving information and materials they could take home
- Having enjoyable activities
- Working with facilitators who were from the community
- Inviting children to attend with their dads
- Making their own books
- Being with other dads and male caregivers

Take-Home Activity Kits

Take-Home Activity Kits, usually aimed at moms, can easily be adapted to appeal to dads. The kits are fun and highly motivating for both parent and child, and they connect children's learning experiences at school with home. They require some thought, planning, and financial resources; however, the benefits are many. Although seen most often in the early elementary grades, they can be very appropriate for use with older students and their families as well.

Although Take-Home Kits are most often organized by classroom teachers, their use can become a whole school project, or work in partnership with the school library. Here are a few hints and suggestions for developing and managing Activity Kits:

- Start a list of kits you want to make. Decide if you will start with one curriculum area or if you will have cross-curricular kits. List the types of materials you hope to put in each kit. It is helpful to start with a great book and build the kit around that.
- Try to keep costs as low as possible. Ask families to donate canvas tote bags, backpacks, lunch boxes, or other suitable containers that are in good condition. Invite them to decorate them with iron-on labels and decorations that you send home for this purpose. Purchase paperback books when possible, as these are less expensive.
- Get together with other teachers in your school or district. It is it easier to share ideas and divide up the work of creating instructions and activities for the kits when a group works together on this kind of project. More lists can be made with less time and energy.
- Be organized. Enclose loose materials in resealable bags or small plastic containers. Write the name of each activity on the kit in paint or marker. Laminate instruction sheets and directions, and attach them to the bag

with yarn or a ring to help keep them from getting lost. Include a checklist of materials in each kit.

- Designate a space. Have a place in your classroom to store the kits and to check the kits in and out. Keep replacement materials here as well.
- Seek volunteers. Find parent volunteers who will help assemble the bags. A group of volunteers may be willing to help examine all the bags once a month and make repairs and replace items if necessary. You may also find one or more parents who will check the bags in for you and sign out new ones. Sometimes older students can be recruited for this purpose.

Most often kits are related to some aspect of the curriculum, such as language arts, science, or math. They are usually organized around a theme or topic in the curriculum area, and contain a book or magazine related to the theme, laminated set of directions for one or more activities, reusable materials to go with one or more of the activities, and a journal for recording comments.

Literacy Kits

Family Literacy Bags are thematic, content-related collections of fiction and nonfiction books with accompanying activities. Their purpose is to connect school and home, as well as to increase parents' knowledge about their children's learning. They are meant to supplement and extend the curriculum while providing opportunities for children to share what they are learning with their family. Books that are interactive, have lots of humor, provide information on a topic, are activity-oriented, or show dads and children doing things together are great motivators for dads to get involved.

Science Kits

Family Science Kits provide a hands-on opportunity to learn about science in a family-oriented, enjoyable way. Each child and his/her family is asked to conduct a simple science experiment at home and bring the results back to share with the class. A variation of this activity asks parents to help children practice a simple experiment at home that they can then demonstrate at school. Parents help fill out a Lab Report for the class science journal. The bag is kept at home for three to four nights. Dads usually enjoy carrying out these experiments with their children.

Math Kits

Hands-on activities and games are a great way to involve dads and to give children extra math practice and academic support. Children are able to manipulate, reflect on, discuss, read, listen, draw, write, and think about previously learned mathematical concepts and share this learning with their families. The games in the kit are usually for multiple players and help overcome math anxiety on the part of both parent and child.

Theme Kits

Activity Kits need not be limited to curriculum subject areas. Some of the best kits are organized around a broad theme or topic, giving you a wider choice of books and activities, ensuring the Kits will have wider appeal. Try to think outside the box to create kits that will have high interest for both child and dad; for example, a building kit, a night sky kit, a design or invention kit, or a car kit will often capture a dad's interest and imagination. See Theme Ideas for Take-Home Activity Kits on page 95.

Dads in Action: Backpacks for Dads Project

The Backpacks for Dads Project was funded through a grant from the provincial teachers union.

The Backpacks for Dads Project was designed to involve dads more actively in their children's homework. Grade 2 teachers worked with the school librarian to design a set of engaging backpacks. Instead of having the bags go home with the children, they decided to house the backpacks in the school library and to open the library one evening each week for two hours. They found that dads were more available between 6:00 and 8:00 p.m., and that they were more likely to read the books and do the activities if they were able to choose the backpack with their child. The backpacks complemented the science program. There were six units, including plants and animals, environmental awareness, rocks and minerals, stars and planets, matter and energy, and motion and forces. A duplicate set of all the bags and several different backpacks for each unit were assembled.

A catchy title for each backpack (e.g., Deep, Down Underground; You Can't Catch Me, etc.) and several related books kept interest high. For example, the Starry, Starry Night backpack contained these books:

- *The Kids Book of the Night Sky* by Ann Love
- *The Zoo in the Night Sky* by Jacqueline Mitton
- *Once Upon a Starry Night* by Jacqueline Mitton
- *How the Stars Fell into the Sky: A Navajo Legend* by Jerrie Oughton and Lisa Desimi

Materials and activities included:

- make-your-own-star-chart pattern
- constellation flash cards
- self-stick glow-in-the-dark stars (for kids to create their own bedroom constellations)
- connect-the-dots constellation templates
- an eight-page blank book for dads and children to record the activities they did together in writing, drawings, or photos.

The backpacks were an instant success. The librarians and teachers held a launch night and had all the backpacks on display. They talked about the project, how it worked, and why they were asking dads to participate. They shared the contents with the dads and the children to heighten interest. Children whose fathers were not at home were encouraged to invite a grandfather or another male relative. At the launch, a backpack was chosen by each dad and signed out for one week.

The teachers were concerned about the children whose dads were not living at home or who were unable to take part. They contacted the families to see if they were interested in allowing their child to participate with a community volunteer who had been carefully selected. With parent permission, the child was then teamed up with a "big brother" volunteer after school to select a bag and do the activities together.

The backpacks resulted in a number of positive spin-offs. The dads initiated more contact with the classroom teacher, usually around some aspect of the backpack activity. They shared information with each other when at the library. They made suggestions for topics to add to the set. They made provisions for exchanging backpacks when they couldn't make it to the library at the designated time. As the backpacks became part of the home routine, the dads contributed more to the blank books and often used digital photography to capture their activities. There were several reasons for the success of the project in the dads' eyes:

- They could choose the backpack they wanted to take home.
- They appreciated the evening at the library where they could exchange bags and talk to other dads.
- They felt they had a better idea of their children's science program through the backpacks.
- They liked having something from their own experience to talk to the teacher about.
- The activities were fun and they felt their children liked doing them with their dad.
- They liked the topics and enjoyed learning along with their child.

Theme Ideas for Take-Home Activity Kits

Incredible Edibles

Include a number of picture books—*Cloudy With A Chance of Meatballs* by Judi Barrett, *Stinky Cheese Man and Other Fairly Stupid Tales* by Jon Scieszka, *Green Eggs and Ham* by Dr. Seuss, *Watch Out For The Chicken Feet in Your Soup* by Tomie dePaola—and longer chapter books, such as *Charlie and the Chocolate Factory* by Roal Dahl.

It's About Time

Include books about telling time, science activities with sundials, and nonfiction books about clocks.

What's So Funny?

The theme of this kit is humor. Fill the bag with joke and riddle books, humorous folk tales such as *What's So Funny Keto?* by Verna Aardema, *Tops and Bottoms* by Janet Stevens, *Some Smug Slug* by Pamela Duncan Edwards.

Dragon Fire

This kit is devoted to dragons. Look for picture books such *as Raising Dragons* by Jerdine Nolan; search the Internet for more. Include books about Chinese New Year and the Dragon Dance, and nonfiction about the Komodo Dragon. A great read aloud for younger children is *My Father's Dragon* by Ruth Stiles Gannette.

Spiders, Bugs, and Creepy Crawlies

The contents of this kit can focus on all sorts of insects. Books with lots of real pictures are best. Include an EyeWitness Video or DVD (e.g., *Butterfly and Moth*). National Geographic has a great reference for children: *My First Pocket Guide to Insects*. Include a viewing jar or magnifying glass.

Weird and Wonderful Weather

You will have no trouble finding lots of books suitable for this theme: *Cloudy With A Chance of Meatballs* by Judi Barrett, *Weather Facts* by Usborne, *Weather At Your Fingertips* by Judy Naylor, *Thunder Cake* by Patricia Polacco, *EyeWitness Weather* by Brian Cosgrove, *The Magic School Bus Inside A Hurricane* by Joanna Cole. You can also include books with science experiments and some materials or a log book in which to record the results. Add a blank calendar for keeping track of the weather.

Ocean Treasures

Books abound for this theme: *The Magic School Bus on the Ocean Floor* by Joanna Cole, *The Sign of the Seahorse* by Graham Base, *Hello Ocean* by Munoz Ryan, *Olive's Ocean* by Kevin Henkes, and *Zoom At Sea* by Tim Wynne-Jones are just a few of the picture books available. Be sure to have some nonfiction as well. Include a treasure bag with shells and beach stones, and an ocean journal.

CHAPTER **6** **Further Connecting Classroom and Home**

This section contains a number of ideas for special events and whole-school activities to complement and extend ongoing classroom initiatives. Whether organized by an individual teacher or teachers at one or more grade levels, or undertaken by a school or an entire district, these initiatives bring dads and their children together in ways that are enjoyable, informative, and engaging for both. They are perfect for garnering community support and partnerships, which is often the key to their success. Each event can be as elaborate as you have the time, energy, and financial support to make it. However, most of these examples require little more than a small group of committed individuals to implement.

Getting Others on Board

When looking to take on a bigger project here are a few tips to help get you started:

- **Consider who else might get involved:** Think about the staff, parents, and community members you know, and make a list of those you think may be interested in the project. Perhaps they have talked to you about the dads' projects you are already doing; perhaps you have heard them say they wished more dads would get involved; perhaps they have a particular talent or interest related to the event you want to undertake. Make a list and add to it as other names come to mind or are recommended to you.
- **Seek community sponsorship:** If funding is needed, start with your school administrator to see what help he/she might be able to offer. Investigate what grants can be obtained from your teachers union or association. Approach local businesses to see if they will make a small donation: when approaching businesses, have a letter ready, on school stationery, that explains the event, outlines who the target population is, and states why it is an important event to support. Be specific about what you want from supporters (e.g., an amount of money, refreshments, etc.). Try not to approach businesses that are already big school sponsors, as they will likely allocate financial support only to the projects they have historically supported. Try some of the smaller businesses who may have previously been overlooked. Approach your school board with a well-written two- or three-page description of the project, including any community support you have obtained thus far; again, be specific about what you want from them. Be sure to list the benefits to the board, to the district, and to student learning.

- **Contact potential partners in person:** Whenever possible, see people in person. Perhaps invite them for coffee. Explain why you feel the event may be of interest to them and how you want them to help. Have several choices of jobs to offer them. Keep the jobs small so potential partners will feel the responsibility won't all fall on their shoulders and, whenever possible, have several helpers assigned to the same job. Try to match the jobs with the person's proximity to the job; for example, if the job is signage, there may be teachers in your building willing to take this on as long as they have a list of what is required, and if the job is broken up among two or more of them. They might also involve their students in the creation of the signs, in putting them up and taking them down.

Book Clubs

Book clubs are as varied as the parents and children who participate; however, having a basic structure to fall back on helps to ensure success.

Book clubs are a great way to involve dads in the literacy development of older children. They encourage both parent and child to read at home, and become a way for parent and child to share some special time together. Book clubs also help children develop important language skills. Book discussions help children practice turn-taking; encourage them to use language to analyze, make predictions, and solve problems; and provide them with opportunities to try out new vocabulary words. In addition, by reading and participating in discussions themselves, dads can provide important language and literacy models for their children.

The key to starting a successful book club depends on a few basic considerations:

- Decide who the target group will be. Will you limit participation to dads whose children are in a particular grade or will you open participation to a group of grades? Sometimes determining a theme or genre in advance (e.g., books about horses, mysteries, science fiction) will help.
- Select books in advance. Put together multiple copies of books that might be appropriate for the book club to read. You can find books through your school or public library, or borrow from other teachers in your school or district. If you have funding, you can purchase books especially for your book club. It is necessary to purchase only one book for each father-child pair.
- Build enthusiasm among the children. Do short promotions to explain what a book club is all about. Have a selection of books that might be read. If children are enthusiastic, they may be able to convince their dads to give it a try.
- Try to make a personal contact with the dads. Telephone the dads of the children who have expressed an interest in the book club. Take the opportunity to explain the benefits to their children and to describe how the club will work. Have a specific date, location, and time in mind for the sessions. Follow up with a invitation handmade by the children.
- Limit the number of participants. Between five and ten dad-child pairs is best. You need enough to have a discussion, but not so many that there won't be enough time for participants to discuss.
- Offer snacks and free books. For a small amount of money, you can provide each dad with a free book. This can be the book the group is going

to read or another one. I like to give a different book as an incentive to keep reading after the book club has ended.

- Have an organizational session. Make expectations clear. Inform dads and children how much they would be expected to read (the number or pages or chapters) and how long they have to read them (one week, two weeks). Explain what they have to do to prepare for each session. Decide on a meeting schedule and the first book the group will read.
- If you are not able to facilitate the book club yourself, you may be able to find a parent, another teacher, or a local librarian who will. If a group of teachers is organizing the club, take turns facilitating the sessions you have planned.

Dads in Action: The Dads and Comics Book Club Project

The Dads and Comics Book Club Project was funded through local fundraising.

The Dads and Comics Book Club Project brought together Grade 4 children and their dads to read and talk about comics and graphic novels. Over the four sessions, for an hour and a half on Friday evenings, dads and children received an assortment of comics and graphic novels donated by used-book stores. The sessions started at 6:00 p.m., which allowed participants to get home at a reasonable hour. A light snack was provided. Each session was held at the local elementary school and facilitated by a local father and his teenage son, who were comic enthusiasts.

Graphic novels and comic books are great motivators for children and dads alike. They get the reader hooked by making links across the books in the series. They are also a genre that dads remember enjoying when they were children. They are nonthreatening and associated with childhood fun and entertainment usually enjoyed outside school. The dads in the project felt very comfortable reading comics. They were familiar with their rapid pace, the importance of the illustrations, the minimal use of print, the opportunity for making sound effects and noises as part of the reading, and the way characters from one book often migrated into another. They were not as familiar with graphic novels, but they recognized some of the same characteristics in this relatively new genre. Their feeling of comfort and familiarity with comics carried over to the graphic novels, and they read them with the same enthusiasm. The children were often surprised with their dad's knowledge of the storyline and characters, particularly of the comic superheroes.

At the final session, the dads and children had the opportunity to make and print out their own comics on the computer using free Internet software designed for this purpose. A father-and-son team with computer skills were recruited to assist with this session. A special two-hour session was allotted for instruction in how to use the program, generating ideas for the comic, creating it and printing it out. A display of the comics was set up in the school library and a "comic convention" was held at a later date to allow the authors to show their books to family and friends. Refreshments were also provided.

The book club achieved several outcomes. The dads demonstrated to their children that they had considerable knowledge about and enthusiasm for this genre. The dads recognized they had a shared interest with their children that led to improved communication. The dads and children were committed to the book club and faithfully attended. They saw themselves as being able to continue on with this activity after the club ended. Participants expressed a number of reasons why they felt this project was a success:

- The project started with something they knew about or were familiar with.
- The facilitators were good role models and demonstrated enthusiasm. It was good to see a father-son facilitator pair.
- They appreciated receiving free comics and graphic novels, and said they would check out the local book stores for more books.
- They liked learning how to use a new computer program and having help to make their own comic.
- Celebrating their comic creations made them feel very proud.

Scavenger Hunts and Book Searches

Everyone loves a treasure hunt, and dads are no exception! Whether the search is online or in a library, school, or community, the game aspect of hunts and searches has wide appeal for dads and their children. These activities can be put together with a minimum expenditure of time, preparation, and sponsorship. Hunts can be informative as well as fun; for example, a library scavenger hunt can get dads into the library and help make them aware of the programs, services, and resources libraries offer families; a science scavenger hunt can help dads and children learn that science is everywhere around them; a treasure hunt around the local community can feature local historical points of interest as well as libraries and museums. Because they are interactive, these activities capture dads' attention, engage their interests, and appeal to their sense of adventure and challenge.

Types of Scavenger Hunts

Type	Features
Traditional	Participants are given a list of items to retrieve and bring back within a designated time limit. Themes can add to the fun: e.g., superhero, recipe ingredients, etc.
Puzzle Piece	Pieces of a jigsaw puzzle are hidden around the designated search area. When all the pieces have been collected and put together, they reveal a question to be answered or a final location to go to.
Photo Scramble	Participants are asked to take photos of their group with particular objects or in specified locations.
Sound Hunt	Instead of retrieving objects, participants are given a list of sounds to record with a tape recorder or other audio recording device.
Combination	You can combine various types of scavenger hunts together and tailor them to your theme: e.g., the list could have situations to photograph as well as objects to retrieve, people to find, clues to solve, facts to discover, puzzles to solve.

Scavenger Hunt Organizer's Checklist

What is the purpose?

Special event	Y	N
Target group	Y	N
Celebration	Y	N

What type?

Traditional	Y	N
Puzzle	Y	N
Photo	Y	N
Sound	Y	N
Combination	Y	N

What are the boundaries?

School	Y	N
Community	Y	N

What items need to be collected? List here.

What are the rules?

Points	Y	N
Prizes	Y	N

How will invitations be distributed?

Students	Y	N
School newspaper	Y	N
Local media	Y	N

There are many web-searches already developed that you can draw on for ideas and inspiration. In addition, if you are looking for more help designing scavenger hunts, you may want to consult a children's party book. Often these ideas can be adapted for school use. The key to successful hunts and searches is in the planning. Use the Scavenger Hunt Organizer's Checklist on page 101 to make sure you have taken all important points into consideration.

Dads in Action: The Education Week Project

The Education Week Book Search Project was funded by the elementary school's home and school association.

A small school used Education Week to launch a book search designed to involve dads and boys in an active and challenging, fun-filled literacy event. A children's book was hidden somewhere in the community. Over the course of a week, clues as to the book's whereabouts went home daily with students of both the elementary and high school, and were posted at the local convenience store and on church bulletin boards.

Teams of families and community members registered at the elementary school and were given a small packet of information. Although open to everyone in the community, each search team had to have at least one male aged 19 or older and one male younger than 19. Teams could guess the book and its whereabouts at any point during the week, and as often as they liked, by including the book's title, its location, their team name, and the date and time of their guess. The final clue went home on Friday; the winning team was announced at a special assembly on the following Monday.

The school found that the book search drew participation from a large number of men and boys. There were more than the obligatory over/under 19-years-old males on the teams. Most often, once one male was recruited, he brought two or three others on board as well. Since the search itself required some knowledge of the local area, and the ability to read a map and solve puzzles, it demanded active participation and drew on the combined skills of the participants. These were skills the dads felt comfortable sharing.

The book search achieved several things. It brought together male community participants across generations as dads, grandparents, and other males in the area were drawn in. The book search became the "talk of the town." It helped dads find a comfortable way to participate in a school-related literacy initiative. The skills and knowledge dads seemed unsure of in one context—the school—became ones they felt capable of sharing in this context. As teams became more and more determined to make sense of the clues, they drew on the skills and knowledge the dads had: some for leadership, some for local history, some for map reading, etc. The teams returned time and again to the clues for confirmation, clarification, and illustration. This allowed dads the support they needed to participate without having to worry about their own literacy level. The collective of the group minimized any individual shortcomings. For many dads, especially those of middle- and high-school children, it was the first time they had participated to such an extent in any school activity. The dads were engaged, enthusiastic, and increasingly confident. The dads in this event felt it was successful because

- The book search was a lot of fun.
- They were "forced" to get involved by the requirement of male participants on each team.

- The time was flexible. It was up to the teams to decide when and how they would get together.
- They didn't have to be good readers or know anything about books in order to participate.
- They liked the team effort.
- They liked being on a team with adults as well as children.

Family Literacy Nights

A Family Literacy Night is a fun-filled, literacy-oriented evening. Usually held at a local school, it is a chance for families to celebrate the joys and benefits of reading and to acquire new information about supporting their children's literacy learning. The structure of these nights varies; they are usually tailored to the interests of the particular school's families. See Family Nights that Dads Enjoy on page 104 for some ideas.

There should be a menu of activities scheduled for Family Literacy Nights that will appeal to all ages. It is important to keep families engaged but not to overload the evening. A few well-chosen activities are best. The ideas listed below can fit with any theme:

- Guest Readers: Recruit local sports stars, police officers, business people, teachers, school custodians, bus drivers, principals, etc. to read aloud a children's picture book, an excerpt of a novel, or a poem during the event.
- Make Something: Hands-on activities, such as making story chains, tongue-twister competitions, and related crafts, are effective.
- Book Swaps: Families are given the chance to add a new book to their personal libraries. Each person brings a book to swap, adults included.
- Dress Up: Make the evening a costume party where parents and children are invited to dress up as their favorite children's book character. They can come in costume or make one on the spot.
- Games: Trivia, jeopardy, and bingo are games that are easily adapted to be about books, authors, and reading in general.
- Stations: Families rotate from one station to the next. The following can be adapted to fit most themes: a puppet theatre for storytelling; a Scrabble table; a continuous-story station, where families help write a story that has already been started; a silly stories centre, where children pick the nouns, verbs, and adjectives from different jars and create sentences; a games table; a make-and-take bookmark station; a place to read books online or on CD.
- Author/Book Celebrations: An author or favorite book can be the focus of the night.
- Contests and Raffles: Donated books make great prizes.

There are several keys to success when organizing a Family Literacy Night. The Literacy Night Organizer's Checklist on page 105 will help you plan.

Sample Family Literacy Night Schedule
5:30 Doors open
5:45–6:45 Celebrity stations
6:45–7:15 Refreshments and book swap
7:15–7:45 Presentation for parents; Activity for children
7:45 Parents rejoin children: raffle draw, hand-outs, thank-yous

Family Nights that Dads Enjoy

Plan a family night for dads around any theme you choose. Below are a few of the more popular ones. Keep this list handy and add to it as you learn of other successful events or think of ones you want to try.

Kitchen Science Night

Prepare kits with the materials to conduct a simple science experiment. If there are several different kits, dads and children can exchange their kit for another once they have completed the experiment. Experiments using everyday or kitchen materials are ideal.

Midnight Turkey Night

Playing off the book *Matthew and the Midnight Turkeys* by Allan Morgan, dads and children make their own sandwiches, write notes to the Midnight Turkeys, and create fanciful recipes. Reading the book at the beginning of the night gets things off to an enthusiastic start.

Ready, Set, Go

Invite dads and children to a night of activities in the gym or outdoors on the playground. Select a number of cooperative games to play that encourage teamwork and collaboration.

Have A Fit

This is a night of fitness activities. Invite the gym teacher or a fitness trainer to lead a variety of simple exercises that dads and children can do. Have some energizing music on hand.

Make-and-Take Night

Dads and children make something together: flying machines out of found materials, bird feeders, boats, small race cars, or other easy-building projects that can be accomplished in an hour are great choices. At the end of the evening, participants take home their creations.

Off to the Races

With cardboard tubes and duct tape, dads and children build a race track for an assortment of small vehicles to travel through.

The Great Paper Airplane Show

Have directions and materials available for making an assortment of paper airplanes. These can be decorated and tested, and then flown. Have books on hand that provide ideas, should dads want to use them for reference and tips.

Literacy Night Organizer's Checklist

Helpers

    Community members ☐

    Family members ☐

    Former students ☐

    Other ☐

Schedule

    Time frame ☐

    Activities ☐

    Snacks ☐

Registration

    Number of participants   _____

    Deadline to register   _____

    Cancellation plan ☐

Sponsors

-
-
-

Incentives

    Goodie bags for children ☐

    Free books ☐

    Raffle tickets ☐

    Coupons ☐

Notes:

Dads in Action: The Buy-a-Book-for-Dad Project

The Buy-a-book-for-Dad Project was funded through the combined partnership of the school, the local book store, and a community service group.

One school decided to focus on dads by using the money they raised at their annual read-a-thon to have dads and their children go to a local book store and choose a book that the dads would like to read to their children. The books were to become part of the Dads Collection and were given a special place in the school library.

An arrangement was made with the bookstore whereby each family was given a set amount to spend on a book or books of their choosing. The school issued a voucher to each family; the amount was determined by dividing the total funds raised by the number of families in the school. It was arranged with the store that the dads and children would be encouraged to come to the store on a designated evening and a Saturday to spend their vouchers. Families who did not have dads at home or who were unable to come were asked to select a book they thought a dad would like to read.

Dads were assisted with their purchasing by the helpful staff. They were encouraged to read aloud to their children as many books as they liked until they found one they wanted to purchase. The dad selecting the book put his name on the voucher along with his child's name and submitted it with the book, which was placed the book into a box behind the check-out. The boxes of books with their vouchers were picked up by the school. If there was any money left over, members of the school staff were invited to spend the remainder.

Over a two-week period following the spending spree, volunteers catalogued the books for the library. They also made out book plates that indicated the name of the dad and child who selected the book. A special sticker of a dad and child was put on the cover of each book. Once all the cataloguing was completed, a Family Literacy Night was held. Families were invited to come to the school and browse all the books that were purchased. A few dads were contacted to speak about why they chose their book and to give a short summary of the book. Members of the local high-school boys basketball team were invited to be celebrity readers.

The project accomplished several goals. A large number of dads participated. Many had never been in a children's bookstore before, and few had ever chosen a book by themselves for their child. They also participated at the Family Literacy Night and spoke with authority about the books they had chosen and why. The dads learned about a wide variety of children's books from the bookstore staff. They showed enthusiasm for the task and conveyed that to their children.

The participants reported that what made the project successful was that

- It was different. They were surprised that they had been given an opportunity to buy books they liked.
- It gave them the opportunity to become familiar with lots of books.
- The bookstore staff was knowledgeable and friendly.
- There was a celebration evening where they could share books with the rest of the family and with other parents.
- It didn't seem like a school event.
- They felt good knowing there were books chosen by dads or for dads. They felt the school was making an effort to include them in their children's learning.

Concluding Thoughts

The dads that I interviewed, as part of a research project on the role dads play in their children's literacy development, said that the most influential source of information for them was the school and, more specifically, their child's teacher. As one of the dads put it:

> When my child's teacher sends home information about anything, I take notice. I don't have to worry about how good it is or if it is going to be good for my child. I figure, she knows and wouldn't send it home if it wasn't any good. (Berand)

Berand, like many other dads, depends on the school to offer quality activities that will benefit his child.

This is an important observation to keep in mind. With a teaching population made up predominantly of women, there is a tendency to think that dads will not take notice or that they will be inclined to ignore activities and events that are organized by female teachers or administrators. This does not seem to be the case. The school and especially the child's teacher have an important role to play in getting the word out.

Just as with any educational undertaking, sharing your ideas with others and having them share their ideas with you enriches the experience for all. Here are a few ways to find and give the support that may be needed as you look for ways to reach out to dads:

- **Network**: Seek out other teachers and administrators who are interested in reaching out to dads. Share information, collaborate on projects, and compare results.
- **Ask for Professional Development:** Contact conference organizers and schoolboard officials responsible for professional development programming, and request workshops on various aspects of interest to you: research, particular initiatives, panel discussions, interagency perspectives, make-and-take, removing barriers, etc.
- **Devote a part of your class website to dads:** Share materials, information, strategies. Create a communications centre on a bulletin board or table outside your classroom with a section that is devoted to dads.
- **Talk it up:** In your local community and in the professional community, talk up the need for reaching out to dads.
- **Make use of new media:** Blogs, face book, podcasts, etc. allow you to reach a wider audience.
- **Get publicity:** If you have a topic that captures the attention of TV and radio personalities, they will be your best allies. A little free advertising goes a long way!
- **Be patient and persistent:** Don't expect to win over dads (or others, for that matter) quickly. It takes time for any change to take hold.
- **Show leadership:** Offer to help others. Let them know what you have done in the form of workshops at local, national, or international conferences.

I'll leave the last word to one of the dads:

> I'm so glad I took part [in the program for dads]. I was nervous at first about what to expect, but I learned so much. And most of all I liked spending time with my daughter. She still talks about it. In fact we both do. It's something only we share—something special—between her and her dad. I like that a lot. Keep them coming!

Appendix: Books to Read Aloud

This list is adapted from the ReadyReaders website.

All of these books are excellent read-aloud choices for children of all ages. With each title is a brief summary.

A Chair for My Mother, Vera B. Williams. A Caldecott Honor book, this is a warm, simple, engagingly illustrated story about a family with strong bonds. A fire destroys their old furniture, and three generations come together—a child, her mother, and her grandmother—to save their money in order to buy a new easy chair.

A Hat for Minerva Louise, Janey Morgan Stoeke. A hen feels cold, but she wants to stay outside in the snow, so she goes searching for warm things. Some of the things she finds are ridiculous (a garden hose, a pot), and even the warm things are funny—mittens on her head and tail.

A-Hunting We Will Go!, Steven Kellogg. A lively, funny song-story with amusing, detailed pictures to read and/or sing aloud. A sister and brother try to put off going to bed by singing a song that takes them on an imaginary trip. They meet a moose and a goose on the loose, a weasel at an easel, and finally—after hugs and kisses—it's off to sleep they go!

All By Myself, Mercer Mayer. Most of the "little critter" books are very popular with preschool children. In this one, the hero learns how to do things like get dressed, brush his teeth, etc., all by himself.

All the Colors of the Earth, Sheila Hamanaka. A wonderful book about diversity. Vocabulary might be a little advanced for younger children.

Animals Should Definitely Not Wear Clothing, Judi Barrett. Especially loved by preschool children and their teachers alike. A laugh-aloud, never-dull book that will be requested over and over again.

Bark, George!, Jules Feiffer. A hysterical, well-written, well-illustrated book by the famous satirist. George, who is a dog, meows! Then he quacks, oinks, and moos. His annoyed and anxious mother takes him to the vet, and guess what? The vet pulls a cat, a duck, a pig and a cow out of George! Now he can bark, but will he? Readers and children alike will laugh out loud at this highly entertaining book.

Barnyard Dance!, Sandra Boynton. If you want a great read-aloud for younger children, get this strongly rhythmical, rhyming book. The robust dancing of nutty farm animals is rudely interrupted by messy monsters. Don't worry: the mess gets fixed. A great book that really illustrates the powerful effects of language.

Big Bad Wolf Is Good, Simon Puttock. The big bad wolf has a bad reputation, so no one will be his friend. The wolf decides to be useful and good, but Mrs. Chicken refuses to let him babysit, because she's afraid he'll eat the little chicks all up. Finally, after the wolf tries to save a baby duck, Mrs. Duck takes a chance on him and invites him to come in for tea. The illustrations of a sad-faced, teary-eyed wolf are quite a change from the usual mean, threatening wolves in storyland. The story also gives a reader a chance to explain that real wolves aren't evil animals at all.

Black on White, Tana Hoban. This book is part of a series of wordless picture books that help children to identify the connections between what they see and what people say (i.e, things and words that name them).

Brown Bear, Brown Bear, What Do You See?, Bill Martin, Jr. The first in a series of books, and probably the best one. A tender rhyming book with beautiful illustrations. Each page features a new animal that sees another one, making us want to turn the page and see it too. Preschoolers will love repeating the rhythmic question on each page. Others in this series: *Polar Bear, Polar Bear, What Do You Hear?*; *Panda Bear, Panda Bear, What Do You See?* (featuring endangered animals).

Can't You Sleep, Little Bear?, Martin Waddell. A tender tale about a little bear who is afraid of the dark, and the big bear who comforts him. First, the big bear brings in lights, and then the two step outside and see the stars at night. A reassuring book for little ones and a good story to quiet children down, this book feels similar in its tone and style to *Goodnight Moon.*

Caps for Sale, Esphyr Slobodkina. A classic and well-respected tale about a peddler with stacks of caps to sell, and the funny things that occur as he tries to sell them. See what happens when he takes a nap under a tree full of monkeys!

Charlie Parker Played Be Bop, Chris Raschka. This book is an outstanding, snappy read-aloud filled with rhythm and jazz and simple (but highly energetic) text and drawings. There are nonsense sounds and real sounds that you and the kids can repeat and share; as a bonus, the book is a great introduction to the great Charlie Parker, to jazz music, and to a couple of musical instruments.

Chewy Louie, Howie Schneider. Chewy Louie is a silly puppy who eats everything in sight. Did he even eat a piece of the front cover of this book? An exciting story with fun-filled illustrations.

Chicka Chicka Boom Boom, Bill Martin, Jr. A wonderfully funny, rhythmical, and suspenseful alphabet book about adventurous letters climbing a coconut tree. It's such fun for the children to repeat the refrain, "chicka-chicka-boom-boom," as the letters tumble down, scramble up, etc. The illustrations are exciting and colorful.

Click Clack Moo: Cows That Type, Doreen Cronin. The idea is hilarious! Some cows in a barn are too cold. They find a typewriter and type a letter to the farmer asking him for electric blankets. The farmer ignores their letter, so they go on strike. Then they type and post a sign that says *No milk today.* In the end, the strike gets resolved with the help of a duck and some open discussion. A non-preachy, lighthearted story with a valuable lesson about using words to work out problems.

Clifford the Big Red Dog, Norman Bridwell. The first in a series of many books about Clifford, a red dog that is bigger than a house, and a little girl named Emily Elizabeth. The very idea of so huge a dog is exciting to the youngest children, and they sit spellbound as Clifford, who doesn't quite understand just how big he is, causes all sorts of mayhem. Some of the Clifford books are a lot less engaging; this one is always a hit!

Cock-A-Doodle Moo, Bernard Most. A rooster loses his voice and can't wake up the farm. The cow tries to help, but can't say, "cock-a-doodle-doo!" After the cow tries "sock-a-noodle-noo" and other laughable variations, she manages a "cock-a-doodle-moo," and everyone finally wakes up. Kids love the funny words and the cartoon drawings.

Corduroy, Taro Gomi. A little girl can't afford to buy Corduroy, a lonely toy bear. But Corduroy thinks he's not adoptable because he's not perfect, as he's missing a button from the strap of his overalls. After the store closes, Corduroy gets down off the shelf and looks for the button all over the store. He has a great adventure, but ends up back on the shelf, sadder than ever, and still with no button. The next day, the little girl returns with money and buys the little bear. She doesn't care if he isn't perfect. She loves him anyway. A beautiful story, beautifully told.

Daddy Is a Doodlebug, Bruce Degen. A young doodlebug describes how he and his father are alike, and explores the things they enjoy doing together.

Dancing in My Bones, Sylvia Andrews. An engaging rhyming book that can be sung to the tune of "If You're Happy and You Know It." The little ones will enjoy reading or singing this book along with you, and they'll like the appealing drawings too.

Dinosaurs Dinosaurs, Byron Barton. A delightful introduction to dinosaurs of various types, shapes, and sizes. The words in the text are fine for younger children, and there are dinosaur names in the back of the book for readers. This book is also a conversation-starter.

Don't Eat the Teacher!, Nick Ward. Sammy the shark is always biting. He eats his school friend, then spits him out. He eats an activity book. He eats his artwork. He even eats the teacher (a lobster). A silly book with funny pictures. No seriousness at all.

Don't Let the Pigeon Drive the Bus!, Mo Willems. A pigeon that longs to drive a bus sees a chance to make its dream come true when the bus driver takes a short break.

Dream Dancer, Jill Newsome. Little Lily dances all the time and everywhere—when she's awake and in her dreams. Then she breaks her leg and despairs until her grandmother gives her a small ballerina doll. Is it Lily or is it her doll who perseveres and dances the way back to health? An intelligent story about hope and the human spirit.

Duck on a Bike, David Shannon. A duck thinks outside the box, and decides to ride a bike. The other farm animals tell him he is wacky, that he'll get hurt, that it's not what dignified animals do, etc. But in the end, the duck's crazy idea doesn't seem so crazy any more. A clever book about the importance of individuality and creativity, even when others may not understand it. Fun-filled illustrations.

Feast for Ten, Catherine Falwell. An appealing counting and sharing book that children will love to read with you. Diversity of characters and family love add to this rich mix.

Feathers for Lunch, Lois Ehlert. Twelve well-known, colorfully and accurately depicted birds and a pet cat go on a non-threatening chase. This book has the added attraction of being a very good introductory nature guide.

Fidgety Fish, Ruth Galloway. A colorfully illustrated adventure story about a little fish with BIG energy! He fidgets endlessly, which kids completely understand... and they enjoy learning the word "fidgety" too.

Fish Eyes: A Counting Book, Lois Ehlert. An imaginative counting book featuring flashy fish floating by. This book can also be used to teach colors and shapes, and it contains some snappy adjectives.

Five Little Monkeys Jumping on the Bed, Eileen Christelow. Mischief and merry-making by five goofy monkeys who all fall off the bed, of course, despite being told repeatedly, "No more monkeys jumping on the bed!" The kids love to wag their index finger back and forth and repeat this refrain, which makes this an engaging read-aloud counting book.

Frog and Toad Are Friends, Arnold Lobel. Five very short stories about two amphibious pals.

Gingerbread Boy, Richard Egiellski. Chased through New York City by famished residents, this delicious cookieboy meets his inevitable end in Central Park. A crictically acclaimed modern retelling of an old classic.

Give the Dog a Bone, Steven Kellogg. About 250 kinds of dogs, some likeable kids, and a few kooky old men give new life to an old counting rhyme that you and children can say or sing. Everyone—from human to critter—has something silly to say or do. Vivacious and terrific read-aloud fun.

Go Away, Big Green Monster!, Ed Emberly. A little hard to find but well worth the trouble! Use the hardcover edition as your read-aloud. Children will cheer after you read this "scary" story about a big green monster, whose features appear and then disappear with each turn of a cut-out page. You shout, "Go away Big Green Monster!" and, one by one, the same features vanish in reverse order. The kids get to tell the monster not to come unless they say so! The pictures are bold and captivating, and kids will want this one again and again.

Go Dog, Go!, P.D. Eastman. A simply lovable love story with simple words that kids will naturally connect with the engaging pictures. A favorite for more than 40 years.

Good Night, Owl, Pat Hutchins. A very sleepy owl just can't get any rest. He tries, but every time he almost falls asleep, some other animal lands in his tree and makes a racket. The owl has finally has enough, and he gets the last screech! A good read-aloud book with snappy descriptions of animal sounds and a guaranteed laugh at the end.

Goodnight Moon, Margaret Wise Brown. What can anyone say about this perfect book except that it is perfect? No child should miss this timeless classic bedtime or quiet-time story.

Green Eggs and Ham, Dr. Seuss. If you read this book quickly and use different voices for the speaking parts of Sam-I-Am and his tormentor, the kids will hang on your every word. A playful classic about a stubborn and very picky eater, who finally agrees to try green eggs and ham—if only to get rid of that pesky Sam.

Gregory the Terrible Eater, Mitchell Sharmat. What would worry goat parents more than a goat child that won't eat goat foods? Instead of shoes, ties, violins and tin cans, Gregory wants eggs and orange juice. What is a good goat parent to do? A funny book that can spark great discussions about food that's good for us and junk food.

Growing Vegetable Soup, Lois Ehlert. "The best soup ever" is in the best how-to introduction to garden veggies. From the planting of the seed, to the picking of the plant, to the preparation of the veggie, to the putting in the pot—this is the complete picture. And what vivid, gorgeous illustrations—almost good enough to eat!

Guess How Much I Love You, Sam McBratney. A sweet story about Nutbrown bunny and his daddy. The little one tries to put off going to bed by coming up with all kinds of ways he loves his dad, but his dad comes up with even better comparisons. Soft and lovely illustrations. A good quiet-down book to read aloud.

Harold and the Purple Crayon, Crockett Johnson. A little boy walks and draws his way through the moonlight with a purple crayon and a big imagination. The drawings are very simple and spare, but this classic story is full of tenderness and feeling.

Harry the Dirty Dog, Gene Zion. Harry is a white dog with brown spots, and he detests baths. To avoid one, he runs away and gets into mischief and dirt, which turns him into a brown dog with white spots. When he goes home, his family doesn't know who he is! A page-turning, funny, lovable read-aloud.

Here Come the Tickle Bugs!, Uncle Sillyhead III. With the refrain, "Here come the tickle bugs," this perfectly foolish book makes kids giggle when they hear it. Full of different-colored silly bugs, this silly book is great fun.

Hi, Pizza Man!, Virginia Walter. A yummy book in which Mom distracts a hungry child by using animal sounds as potential greetings for the pizza-delivery person. A very clever book that works wonderfully as a read-aloud.

Home for a Bunny, Margaret Wise Brown. An oldie but goodie. A little bunny looks high and low for a home. Sometimes, the place is inaccessible. Sometimes, the current occupant won't share. But, finally, the bunny meets another bunny who invites him to share a home under a stone. Lovely illustrations with lots of opportunity to point out details.

Honey I Love, Eloise Greenfield. A highly appealing rhyming book about childhood pleasures, with delightful illustrations of the happy African-American child who experiences them. This positive, beautiful book is a wonderful read-aloud.

How Do Dinosaurs Say Goodnight?, Jane Yolen. This wonderfully written and illustrated book is the first and best in a series of books that use dinosaurs to teach good behavior and coping skills. A fun-filled, meaningful book.

I Love You, Stinky Face, Lisa McCourt. In this book and its companion, *I Miss You, Stinky Face*, children find a feeling of safeness. This highly recommended book is all about a mother's unconditional love.

I Stink!, Kate & Jim McMullan. Kids are crazy about this strange garbage truck with its big mouth and its gross appetite for stinky stuff. How can anyone resist? Incidentally, they'll learn to appreciate what garbage trucks do for us, but most of all they'll get a kick out of copying this brash truck as it burps and growls its way through its rounds.

I Was So Mad, Mercer Mayer. The whole series of "little critter" books is enjoyed by children. In this book, they can easily relate to a little guy who isn't allowed to do some things he would like very much to do—like tickling the goldfish. The very expressive faces of the characters in this series are especially appealing to young children.

If You Give a Mouse a Cookie, Laura Numeroff. This is the first in a series of comical misadventures and tongue-in-cheek lessons about cause and effect. All of the books in this series feature a boy who gets into hysterical situations that lead to other hysterical situations. He learns that taking care of the demands of a needy animal can be quite exhausting!

I'm Gonna Like Me: letting off a little self-esteem, Jamie Lee Curtis. What makes this book fun is the illustrations, which are sure to make children giggle. What makes the book worthy is the self-acceptance message that it conveys.

Is Your Mama a Llama?, Deborah Guarino. Children learn some interesting facts about animals from this delightfully illustrated, award-winning book with its simple questions and rhyming answers.

It Looked Like Spilt Milk, Charles G. Shaw. A delightful book that engages children in an imaginative guessing game. A white object changes its shape on every page. And on every page, that shape looks like something familiar, but it's not that thing at all. Not until the end do we learn what it actually is!

It's the Bear, Jez Alborough. This is one of those scary-yet-silly rhyming books that children enjoy. A bear smells the food from a picnic of a child and his mother. The child hides inside the picnic basket, but his oblivious mom doesn't notice the bear—until he takes the pie. In the end, the bear runs one way and the people run the other way. The illustration at the end will make everyone laugh.

Kitten's First Full Moon, Kevin Henkes. Winner of the Caldecott Medal, this lovely book tells the story of a persistent little kitten who thinks the moon is a bowl of milk and futilely tries all sorts of ways to get it. In the end, she learns there's no place like home to fulfill her heart's desire.

Leaf Man, Lois Ehlert. This books traces the possible journeys of a Leaf Man who blew away. On each page, brightly colored leaves in the shapes of animals and other objects fly wherever the Leaf Man must blow. The book not only encourages small children to think about ways to arrange leaves they might collect in fall, but the endpapers name various kinds of leaves. A spectacular nature book.

Leo the Late Bloomer, Robert Kraus. Poor little Leo the lion just can't do anything right. He can't read or write, and he's a messy eater. This worries Leo and his watchful father, but not his mother. She urges patience, and in due time Leo blooms! Captivating, expressive characters, a little suspense, and a happy ending please everyone.

Lucy's Picture, Nicola Moon. A sensitive and beautifully made book about individuality, creativity, beauty, giving, and love. Lucy's grandfather is blind, and Lucy wants to make him a picture he can "see" with his hands. So while her classmates are painting pictures, Lucy's teacher encourages her to follow her own muse. By pasting objects with different textures onto paper, Lucy makes a collage that her grandfather enjoys.

Machines at Work, Byron Barton. During a busy day at the construction site, the workers use a variety of machines to knock down a building and begin constructing a new one.

McDuff Comes Home, Rosemary Wells. This book is part of a series about the adventures of McDuff, a cute little terrier. In this book, he runs after a rabbit and gets lost in the process. Luckily, a motherly lady with a motorcycle sticks him in her side car and takes him back home. The story and vivid illustrations delight children, and McDuff is a very appealing character.

Mice Squeak, We Speak, Tomie dePaola. A simple, clever, highly praised rhyming book featuring the sounds that animals make and what we do differently (i.e., speak). Colorful, full-page, carefully considered illustrations and text.

Mike Mulligan and His Steam Shovel, Virginia Lee Burton. This classic story teaches children that where there's a will, there's away. Mike Mulligan (and his steam shovel Mary Ann) have made tunnels through mountains, giant holes in which tall buildings sit, and canals for boats; but now, there is electricity and gasoline, so no one seems to want to dig things with a steam shovel.

Mirandy and Brother Wind, Pat McKissack. A gorgeously illustrated, award-winning story about a kind little girl and her clumsy friend, who want to win a dance contest. Mirandy's kindness to her friend helps her triumph, because she is able to capture Brother Wind, who helps them dance beautifully together.

Mouse Count, Ellen Stoll Walsh. What she did for colors in *Mouse Paint*, the author does for numbers here. An exciting story about a blue snake who captures ten tiny mice, some while they're sleeping, one while it's hiding. He sticks them in a jar and plans to eat them, of course; but the ten little mice outwit him, one by one, as we count back from ten. A page-turner and a counting book in a colorful package.

Mouse Paint, Ellen Stoll Walsh. One of the best read-aloud books to teach children about colors. Three peppy white mice jump into jars of yellow, red, and blue paint and then jump out again, creating puddles of paint. They dance and splash their way through the pages of the book, mixing up colors and creating exciting new colors. Brightly colored illustrations and lively characters hold children's attention beautifully.

Mr. Brown Can Moo, Can You?, Dr. Seuss. Oh, the wonderful things Mr. Brown can do! And the amazing sounds he can make! He can make the sounds of a popping cork, a klopping horse, a goldfish kissing, thunder booming, eggs frying… An irresistible, repeat-after-me book that little ones relish!

My Family Plays Music, Judy Cox. A delightful, award-winning book to introduce musical instruments and type of music to children. Everyone in this rainbow of a family is a wonderful musician, and each one plays a different instrument and a different kind of music, making a rainbow of sounds. Bring along a few of the easy-to-carry smaller instruments and let the children help you read this one aloud!

My Friend Bear, Jez Alborough. A warm, gentle story about loneliness, friendship, and love. A lonely little boy with a teddy bear is walking through the woods when he spies a very large teddy bear. Soon an enormous real bear appears, and the frightened little boy holds out his teddy bear and pretends that it—not he—is doing the talking. But the real bear is lonely too, and soon the boy, the bear, and their teddy bears are laughing together and becoming friends.

My Friend Rabbit , Eric Rohmann. Something always seems to go wrong when Rabbit is around, but Mouse lets him play with his toy plane anyway because he is his good friend.

My Little Sister Ate One Hare, Bill Grossman. A goofy, laugh-out-loud book with a storyline that resembles the old song, "I Know an Old Lady Who Swallowed a Fly." This book works best with children old enough to get the silly jokes and even sillier pictures.

My Truck Is Stuck!, Kevin Lewis/Daniel Kirk. This is a hilarious story with very funny pictures. A couple of dogs in baseball caps are driving a dump truck full of bones, and the truck gets stuck in a pothole. The doggy drivers flag down one vehicle after another, but—alas—the truck stays stuck until a tow truck comes to the rescue. In the meantime, some sneaky prairie dogs (who made the pothole in the first place) run off with the cargo.

Oh, A-hunting We Will Go, John Langstaff. It's the old folk song decorated with fun-filled pictures and featuring verses both old and new. The book comes with guitar and piano music. Children might even add their own verses!

Old Black Fly, Jim Aylesworth. An unusual, very funny alphabet book. Family members chase a fly that zips through the house and through the alphabet as it wreaks havoc. The book also has energetic, colorful drawings and an attention-holding, strong rhythmic chant that children can repeat after the reader at the end of each rhyme.

On Mother's Lap, Ann Herbert Scott. An updated, nicely illustrated story about the expansiveness of love. In a cold, sparsely furnished space, a little boy gets his blanket and toys and climbs into his mother's lap. Then his baby sister cries and, to the boy's dismay, his mother wants to bring her to the rocking chair too. It's crowded but it's warm, and there is enough room for him after all.

On the Day You Were Born, Deborah Frasier. A beautiful book with a message about the uniqueness of every child and the place of each of us in the universe. Captivating illustrations fill this book that reinforces self-esteem.

Over in the Meadow, Jane Cabrera. We love this paticular version of the popular song-poem, mainly because the illustrations, which look like finger painting, are so wonderful.

Peek-A-Moo!, Marie Torres Cimarusti. A lift-the-flap book that is sure to be a read-aloud hit. Odd little animals play peek-a-boo with the children you read to. They'll want to hear this one again!

Peekaboo Kisses, Barney Salzman. A loving lift-the-flap, touch-and-feel book. The illustrations are vivid and bright, and the very young will love the textures of the animals under the flaps. At the end, the flap reveals a mirror and ME!

Planting a Rainbow, Lois Ehlert. This glorious book uses vivid colors to explain and show how seeds gradually grow into different plants, each with its own unique flower. A terrific way to teach a young child about how plants and flowers grow, each in its unique way.

Polar Bear Night, Lauren Thompson. A beautifully illustrated award-winner.

Popcorn: A Frank Asch Bear Story, Frank Asch. A bear invites all his friends to a Halloween party, and one by one they show up with a gift of popcorn! Soon, the the whole house fills up with popcorn.

Rainbow Fish, Marcus Pfister. The celebrated story of a richly endowed, lonely fish, who learns that giving things to others brings happiness. Rainbow Fish has an abundance of sparkly scales, and the other fish have none. When a wise octopus suggests that his selfishness is to blame for his loneliness, Rainbow Fish changes his ways.

Saturday Night at the Dinosaur Stomp, Carol Diggery Shields. As every kid knows, dinosaurs are really party animals, and these do all kinds of fun-filled dances (like the Triassic Twist). Colorful, entertaining, and a fun-filled read-aloud. Wait until the kids accompany you by shouting, "Boomalacka boomalacka! Whack! Whack! WHACK!"

Shake My Sillies Out, Raffi. This is a great book to read or sing aloud and get the wigglies and squirmies out! Vivacious illustrations and a lot of fun.

Sheep in a Jeep, Nancy E. Shaw. This is one of those goofy, imaginative stories that delight kids. With its Seuss-like rhymes and outrageously funny pictures, this is a book destined for long-term survival, even if you may question the survivability of the dumb sheep in the jeep.

Shoo Fly!, Iza Trapani. An appealing song or story to sing or read aloud. The illustrations are captivating and the tale of the struggle between a mouse and a fly is entertaining.

Silly Sally, Audrey Wood. Unabashedly rhyming, read-aloud silliness involving a silly girl who goes to town in a silly way—walking backwards, upside-down. She's joined by a pig doing an upside down jig and other silly animals, but all of them eventually end rightside-up.

Sleepy Bears, Mem Fox. Another award-winning book to help every child go to sleep. A mother bear and her little ones snuggle in a big bed to go to sleep for the winter. The mother bear invents a simple, lovely, imaginative story in rhyme that appeals to the individuality of each of her cubs. There's a fairy-tale rhyme for one little cub, a circus rhyme for another, an adventure rhyme for a third, and so on. Sweet dreams... especially on cold winter days.

Snowballs, Lois Ehlert. In this great read-aloud book for a gloomy winter's day, we watch the construction of a snow family, including people and pets—all beautifully dressed up. The unique, detailed illustrations are bright and engaging, and there's an extra bonus: a recipe for popcorn balls!

Snowmen at Night, Caralyn Buehner. A child wonders why a snowman looks so droopy in the morning, and then gets the answer: the snowman was out playing all night—throwing snowballs, drinking cocoa, and generally cavorting with friends. No wonder he's such a mess!

Somewhere Today—A Book of Peace, Shelley Moore Thomas. A simple, engaging book about caring, sharing, and friendship. Wonderful photography shows young children of all races and ages involved in helping other people, young and old. The book ends with the gentle suggestion that every child can do little things to help make the world a better place.

Swimmy, Leo Lionni. Swimmy is a little fish who is dark, while all the other little fish are light. In this appealing story, Swimmy solves a big problem—how to stop the big fish from eating the little fish. A natural leader, Swimmy gets the little fish to unite into a formation that makes them look like one gigantic fish. Then he places himself in the position of the eye of the gigantic fish. United in this way, the little fish can survive. Cleverly conceived and very popular.

Sylvester and the Magic Pebble, William Steig. Sylvester the donkey finds a magic pebble and unthinkingly wishes he was a rock when frightened by a lion. Although safe from the lion, Sylvester cannot hold the pebble to wish himself back into a donkey.

Tacky the Penguin, Helen Lester. Tacky is not a proper, go-along penguin. But it's nutty Tacky who figures out how to fool the hunters who want to capture all of the penguins. The little lesson about the value of thinking for oneself is brightly illustrated and the characters are very expressive.

Ten, Nine, Eight, Molly Bang. A Caldecott Award-winning, beautifully illustrated book in which a little girl and her daddy have fun playing a rhyming game when it's the little one's bedtime.

That Toad is Mine, Barbara Shook Hazen. Two boys who are good friends usually share everything. But when they happen onto a little toad, both of them really want it! What happens next is amusing and a good lesson about sharing. Colorful, exciting pictures will have the kids wanting to know what happens next.

The Big Blue Spot, Peter Holwitz. A big blue spot feels lonely and looks for a friend. In the process, the blue spot meets spots of many other colors. Simply written, with a "what happens next?" plot, this is an excellent book about colors and about diversity too.

The Colors of Us, Karen Katz. A wonderfully told, loving story about a little girl whose friends have skins the delicious colors of cinnamon, ginger, chocolate, honey, pizza, peaches. A great book about the greatness of diversity.

The Doorbell Rang, Pat Hutchins. Two children plan to share a dozen cookies between them (six apiece), but then the doorbell rings, and two more children come in (three apiece now!). But that doorbell just keeps on ringing, and kids, cats, mops, kitchen stuff, bikes, and all sorts of clutter add to the fun! Oh no! Now there are more children than cookies! But wait, here comes Grandma…

The Eensy Weensy Spider, Mary Ann Hoberman. This gorgeously illustrated retelling is one that the youngest children will love. It's a feast for the eyes, and you can read or sing it. It strays from the original song, but it in lovely ways.

The Foot Book, Dr. Seuss. Opposites certainly attract in this funny classic about left, right, up, down, wet, dry, and other feet.

The Grouchy Ladybug, Eric Carle. A grouchy bug with a nasty disposition learns how to behave in this brightly illustrated book. It's best to get the hardback copy with die-cut pages to read to a group. A great teaching book, too, to talk about manners, to compare sizes, and to discuss the concept of time.

The Gruffalo, Julia Donaldson. A little mouse tries to keep a fox from eating him by inventing a story about meeting a gruffalo for lunch. Does the fox believe there is such a thing as a gruffalo? A funny, adventurous, wonderful read-aloud that kids love.

The Itsy Bitsy Spider, Iza Trapani. A delightfully illustrated and conceived version of this little rhyme, which will work best with the youngest children. This version will let you ask "What happens next?" Our little spider not only climbs up and gets washed out of the waterspout, but he then climbs unsuccessfully up a kitchen wall, into a yellow pail, and onto a rocking chair. Finally, he climbs a tree and succeeds in spinning a web. A happy ending and a good example of "try, try again."

The Kissing Hand, Audrey Penn. A little racoon is afraid to go to school, because he thinks he'll be lonely without his mother. His wise mother kisses the palm of his hand, and the little raccoon feels her kiss travel up his arm and into his heart. She tells him that if he feels lonely without her, he will feel her kiss by pressing the Kissing Hand. In a touching climax, the little raccoon gives his mother his own Kissing Hand, so that she won't be lonely without him either.

The Little Engine That Could, Watty Piper. This classic story is forever new. Get the version with the original text and illustrations if you can. An engine is pulling a train up a mountain to deliver toys and treats to children on the other side. It's very hard for him, but he tries and tries. And because he thinks he can, he succeeds!

The Little Mouse, the Red Ripe Strawberry and the Big, Hungry Bear, Audrey and Don Wood. The full-page illustrations, sound effects, and what-happens-next story will grab every child's attention. A frightened little mouse tries to keep a big, hungry bear from getting the red, ripe strawberry that the little mouse has just picked.

The Little Old Lady Who Was Not Afraid of Anything, Linda Williams. A great "scary" silly story for October or any other time. The heroine is a fearless little old lady, who has to handle various articles of clothing and a pumpkin head that are chasing her. The text is funny; the rhythm is catchy; and the illustrations are engaging.

The Mixed Up Chameleon, Eric Carle. A chameleon is thrilled to learn that he can change his shape and color to conform to the different colors and shapes of many zoo animals. But then he starts looking like all of them at one time, and he learns that he also needs to reshape and recolor his ambitions.

The Monster at the End of This Book, Jon Stone. This funny page-turner features Grover of Sesame Street, who keeps imploring us NOT to turn the pages, because there's a monster at the end of the book. Of course, that makes the children want to turn the pages all the more. Guess who is at the end of the book?

The Napping House, Audrey and Don Wood. A great classic book to read after naps! This is a tale of relaxed people and animals who climb into a bed one by one. They are planning to join Grandma and take a nap; but the last one into bed is a flea with other plans! Amusing illustrations lighten and brighten as this sleepy book wakes up.

The Old Woman and Her Pig, Eric A. Kimmel. An updated folk story about an old woman trying to get her stubborn pig to come along. She enlists the help of a dog, a cat, a rat, etc. Children will love this rhythmic, cumulative read-aloud with its zany illustrations.

The Perfect Purple Feather, Hannoch Piven. Unusual, quirky illustrations and an imaginative rhyming story make this a sure winner. A little boy finds a purple feather, and all sorts of oddly-made critters want it for all sorts of unusual purposes.

The Pig in the Pond, Martin Waddell. A dare-to-be-different tale, as well as a fun-filled book to read to children. Although pigs don't swim, Neligan is awfully hot. She decides that the ducks and geese have it right and jumps into the pond too. So do all the other farm animals and the farmer! Silliness and something more…

The Right Number of Elephants, Jeff Sheppard. An unusual, riotous counting book. The book counts backwards from ten to one, with quirky text and big, full-of-life color illustrations.

The Snowy Day, Ezra Jack Keats. A 1963 Caldecott Award-winner, this beautiful classic is the simple story of a little boy who wakes up and discovers the wonders of a snowy city day. Keats' collages are remarkable for their simple, calm beauty and artistry, which mirror the child's joy in making snow angels and enjoying the snow.

The Sun Is My Favorite Star, Frank Asch. A little child tracks the journey of the sun through the day and relates to it both as a and as a big, warm, wonderful object of curiosity and wonder. Glorious illustrations make this a winner.

The Teeny Tiny Woman, Jane O'Connor. A clever, classic ghost story for pre-schoolers. A teeny-tiny woman on a teeny-tiny walk finds a teeny-tiny bone and takes it home to make a teeny-tiny pot of soup. That's when then the silliness and spookiness take over. An especially fun book to read to children in October.

The True Story of the 3 Little Pigs, Jon Scieszka. When Alexander Wolf is framed, he seeks justice and tells his own version of the story of the Three Little Pigs. Children will love this amusing rendition of the classic fairy tale.

The Very Busy Spider, Eric Carle. The spider begins with a few silk strands and, by the end of the book, she has created a complex work of art. Children will enjoy the tactile nature of this book and Eric Carle's vivid, expressive pictures.

The Very Hungry Caterpillar, Eric Carle. This is a wonderful, award-winning book, brightly illustrated, about a caterpillar who eats its way through the days of the week. If you read it to more than one child, try using a big version of this book, because its clever cut-outs would otherwise be difficult to see and manipulate.

The Wing on a Flea, Ed Emberly. An enticing book about circles, rectangles, and triangles and all the things they might be—both separately and in combination.

There's an Alligator under My Bed, Mercer Mayer. Another in the series of delightful books about unusual critters in a chid's bedroom, this book is generally considered the best in the series. Yes, there is an alligator under the bed but, like the monster in the closet, what we imagine is far scarier than what is actually there.

Very Hairy Harry, Edward Koren. A funny book in which a barber tells hairy Harry all the advantages of being hairy. They include being able to hide your favorite things on your body, having your dog look like he's part of you, and being able to forgo winter clothes.

Waiting for Wings, Lois Ehlert. Another amazing book by the author of *Chicka Chicka Boom Boom*. Breathtaking illustrations fill every page of this informative book about the life cycle of the butterfly. The text is a simple rhyme that echoes the gentleness of a butterfly. There are also facts about butterflies, including their names, which make this book interesting for older children too.

Watch Out! Big Bro's Coming, Jez Alborough. A funny-scary story that children adore. The jungle animals are terrified and hide, because they hear that Big Bro is coming. Little mice venture out and affirm the fact, which scares them even more. But aren't they all embarrassed when Big Bro shows up? Big pages and big, bright ink illustrations make this book a great read-aloud.

We're Different We're the Same, Bobbi Kates. A very good book on the subject of diversity and self-esteem.

What! Cried Granny, Kate Lum. A funny story about a little boy, who makes up all kinds of zany excuses explaining why he can't go to bed yet, and his creative, nattily dressed grandmother, who goes to great lengths to give him no other excuse. Even though she chops down a tree to make him a bed and does other clever and superhuman things to satisy his every stated need, the little boy manages to find enough excuses to last the whole night.

When Daddy's Truck Picks Me Up, Jana Novotny Hunter. A little boy eagerly waits for his father to pick him up from school in his big tanker truck.

Where the Wild Things Are, Maurice Sendak. One of the best scary-funny books every written. Max makes mischief and gets sent to his room without supper. In his imagination, the room turns into an ocean on which he sails away to a forest filled with wild things. Max tames them and becomes their king, but he eventually decides to sail back home.

Where's Spot?, Eric Hill. Children love this classic book about a dog, and it's now been republished in brighter colors.

Where's the Baby?, Cheryl Christian. A lift-the-flap book with pictures of babies.

Who Is Driving?, Leo Timmers. Guess which animal is driving each of seven vehicles, then find out their destinations and the sounds the vehicles make.

Who Took the Cookies from the Cookie Jar?, Bonnie Lass. Children love this famous who-done-it. You can read it aloud, read along with children, sing it with them, and use it to play a circle game. (The melody and the game are printed at the front of the book.) The illustrations are colorful and can be used to teach the names of the various animals who may have taken the cookies.

Whoever You Are, Mem Fox. A simple book with universal appeal, this book tells our youngest children that there are other children all over the world who may look and live differently, but who are all the same inside. The illustrations are as beautiful as the message.

Why Mosquitos Buzz in People's Ears: A West African Tale, Verna Aardema. A West African folk story about a mosquito, whose lies cause one strange thing after another to happen until finally, the sun itself stops rising. The artwork in this book is beautiful and captures the heat of a West African day and the velvety darkness of night. Little kids like pointing out a tiny pink bird that happens to be in every scene, and they love the silly sounds that the animals make.

Professional Resources

Allen, JoBeth (2007) *Creating Welcoming Schools: A practical guide to home-school partnerships with diverse families.* International Reading Association.

Booth, David (1992) *Stories to Read Aloud.* Markham, ON: Pembroke.

— (2002) *Even Hockey Players Read: Boys, literacy and learning.* Markham, ON: Pembroke.

Botrie, Maureen and Wenger, Pat (1992) *Teachers & Parents Together.* Markham, ON: Pembroke.

Corgill, Ann Marie (2008) *Of Primary Importance: What's essential in teaching young writers.* Portland, ME: Stenhouse.

Diehn, Gwen (2006) *Making Books that Fly, Fold, Wrap, Hide, Pop-up, Twist and Turn.* New York, NY: Lark.

Endrizzi, Klassen (2008) *Becoming Teammates: Teachers and families as literacy partners.* National Council of Teachers of English.

Flouri, E. & Buchanan, A. (2004) "Early father's and mother's involvement and child's later educational outcomes." *British Journal of Educational Psychology*, Vol. 74, 141–153.

Gadsden, V. (2003) "Expanding the concept of 'family' in family literacy: Integrating a focus on fathers." In Devruin-Parecki, A. & Krol-Sinclair, B. (Eds.), *Family Literacy: From theory to practice*, 86–125.

Gear, Adrienne (2007) *Reading Power: Teaching students to think while they read.* Markham, ON: Pembroke.

— (2008) *Nonfiction Reading Power: Teaching students how to think while they read all kind of information.* Markham, ON: Pembroke.

Hauss, Monty & Hauss, Laurie (2005) *Words That Cook! Parenting With Children's Books.* DVD Series, Shows 1–6. International Reading Association.

Hill, Bonnie (2007) *Supporting Your Child's Literacy Learning: A Guide for Parents.* Portsmouth, NH: Heinemann.

Houssin, F. & Ramadier, C. (2003) *The Big Book of Car Games.* New York, NY: Black Dog & Leventhal Publishers.

Kirkland, L., Aldridge, J. & Kuby, P. (2007) *Integrating Environmental Print Across the Curriculum, PreK–3: Making literacy instruction meaningful.* New York, NY: Corwin Press.

Literacy Begins At Home. Brochure Series. International Reading Association.

Miller, Debbie (2002) *Reading with Meaning: Teaching comprehension in the primary grades.* Portland, ME: Stenhouse.

— (2008) *Teaching with Intention: Defining beliefs, aligning practice, taking action, K–5.* Portland, ME: Stenhouse.

Ortiz, R. (2000) "The many faces of learning to read: The role of fathers in helping their children develop early literacy skills." *Multicultural Perspectives*, Vol. 2(2), 10–17.

Peterson, Shelley Stagg & Swartz, Larry (2008) *Good Books Matter*. Markham, ON: Pembroke.

Raphael, Taffy et al. (2002) *Book Club: A Literature-Based Curriculum*. International Reading Association.

— (2004) *Book Club Plus! A Literacy Framework for the Primary Grades*. International Reading Association.

Richmond, H. & Miles, C. (2004) *Boys' and Girls' Literacy: Closing the gap*. Lakeville, NB: Karen Love.

Rowsell, Jennifer (2006) *Family Literacy Experiences*. Markham, ON: Pembroke.

Seeger, Pete & Jacobs, Paul (2001) *Pete Seeger's Storytelling Book*. New York, NY: Harcourt Trade.

Stile, S. & Ortiz, R. (1999) "A model for involvement of fathers in literacy development with at-risk and exceptional children." *Early Childhood Education Journal*, Vol. 26(4), 221–224.

Thompson, Terry (2008) *Adventures in Graphica: Using comics and graphic novels to teach comprehension, 2–6*. Portland, ME: Stenhouse.

Tomecek, Steve (2006) *Sandwich Bag Science: 25 easy, hands-on activities that teach key concepts in physical, earth, and life sciences—and meet the science standards*. New York, NY: Scholastic, Inc.

Trelease, Jim (2001) *The Read Aloud Handbook, 5th ed.* New York, NY: Penguin.

Van Horn, Leigh (2008) *Reading Photographs to Write with Meaning and Purpose*. International Reading Association.

Index